SHOE-DLES TOO

by

PATRICIA BURKE

Artist of all images created within this book, including the cover art, are the creation of and doodled exclusively by, Patricia Burke.

~Cover Colorist~

Joyce Young

ISBN-13: 978-0997595956

~Shoe-dles Too Coloring Team~

Charlotte Schroeder Beeston
Dana La Porte
Debbie West Cummings
Dee Dee Boseman
Elisabeth Anderson
Jennifer Preston
Jennifer Nicole Scarabin
Joyce Young
Kelly Deuber Taylor
Lina Weikel
Marian Radius
Michelle A Turner
Patty Burke
Shannon Woodford Schuler
Shawn Hallenbeck

Ladies, you've made it so much easier for me to create. I cannot express how much I have appreciated your beautiful pages as well as your feedback. Your help has been, as always, exemplary. I don't ever want to have to do this without you.
Each of you, my coloring team, have been so wonderfully gracious and generous to me and what I do.
I cannot express my gratitude nearly enough.
All I can say is, thank you. Thank you all so very much.

Find my Coloring Books and Pages, below

My Website- **https://www.coloradoodle.com**
Find my Books Here- **https://www.amazon.com/patriciaburke**
Digital Downloads Here- **https://www.gumroad.com/coloradoodle**
Facebook Artist Page Here- **https://www.facebook.com/coloradoodle**
Facebook Fan Group Here-
https://www.facebook.com/groups/colormydoodles/

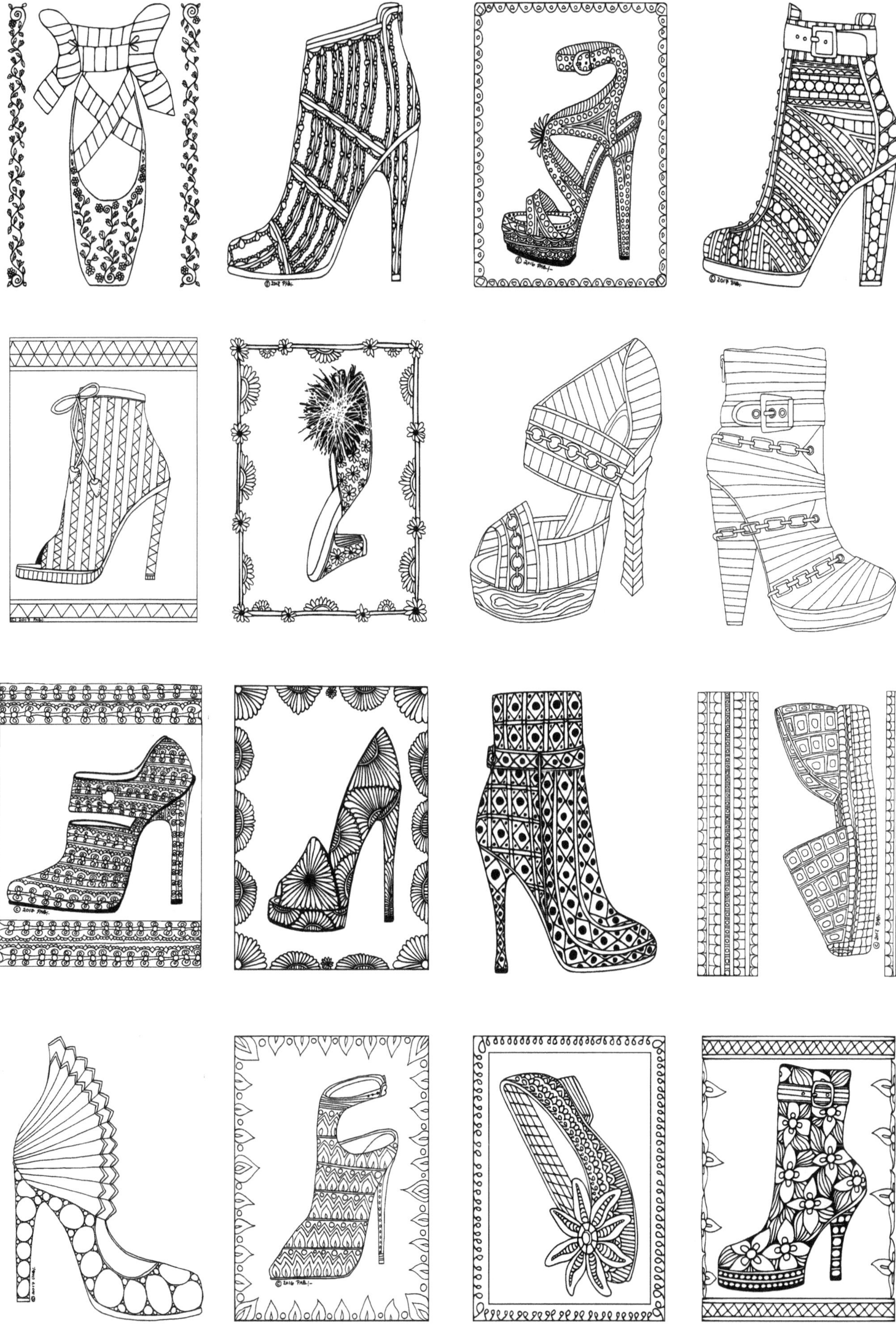

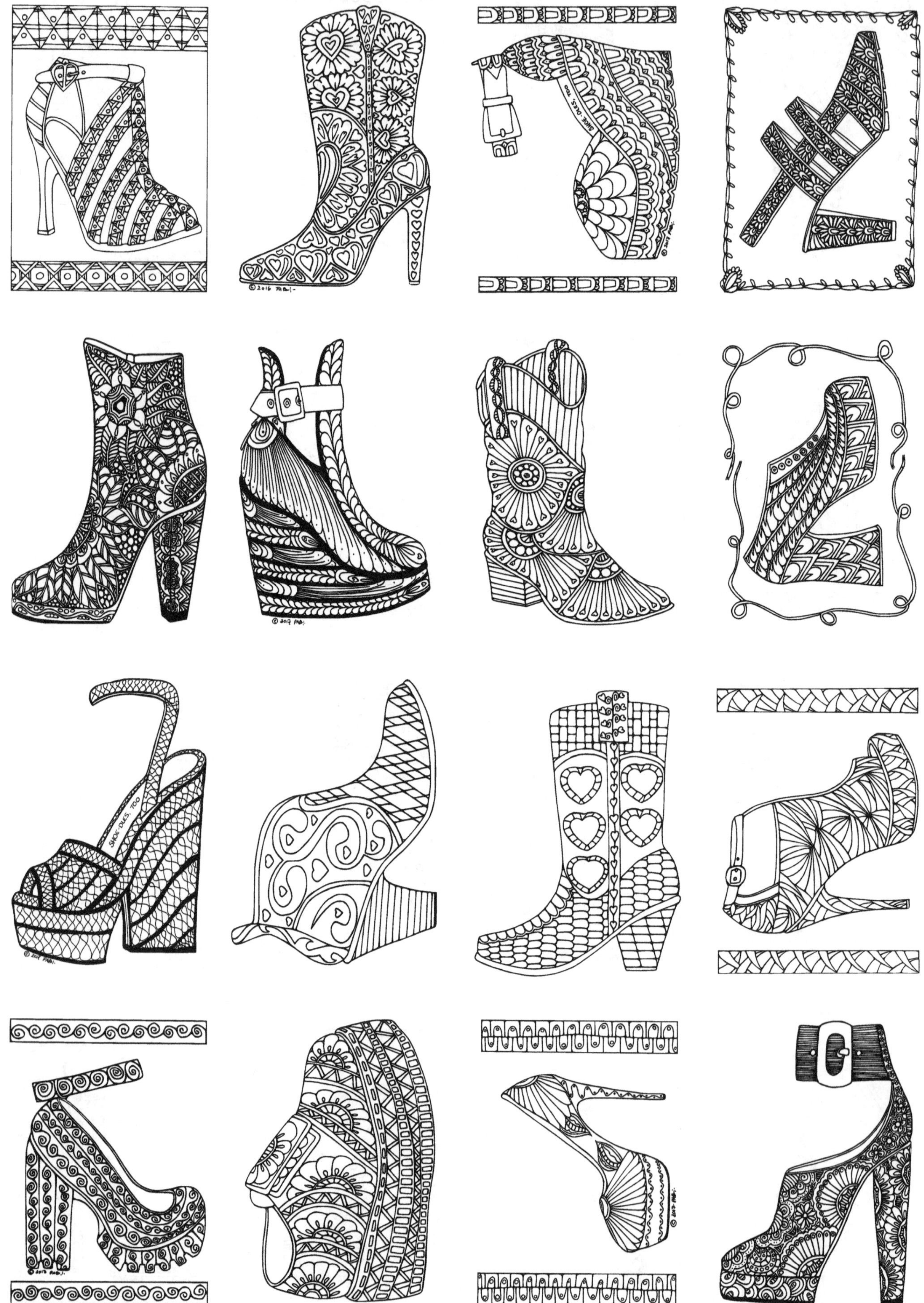
SHOE-DLES, TOO

This Book Belongs To

___

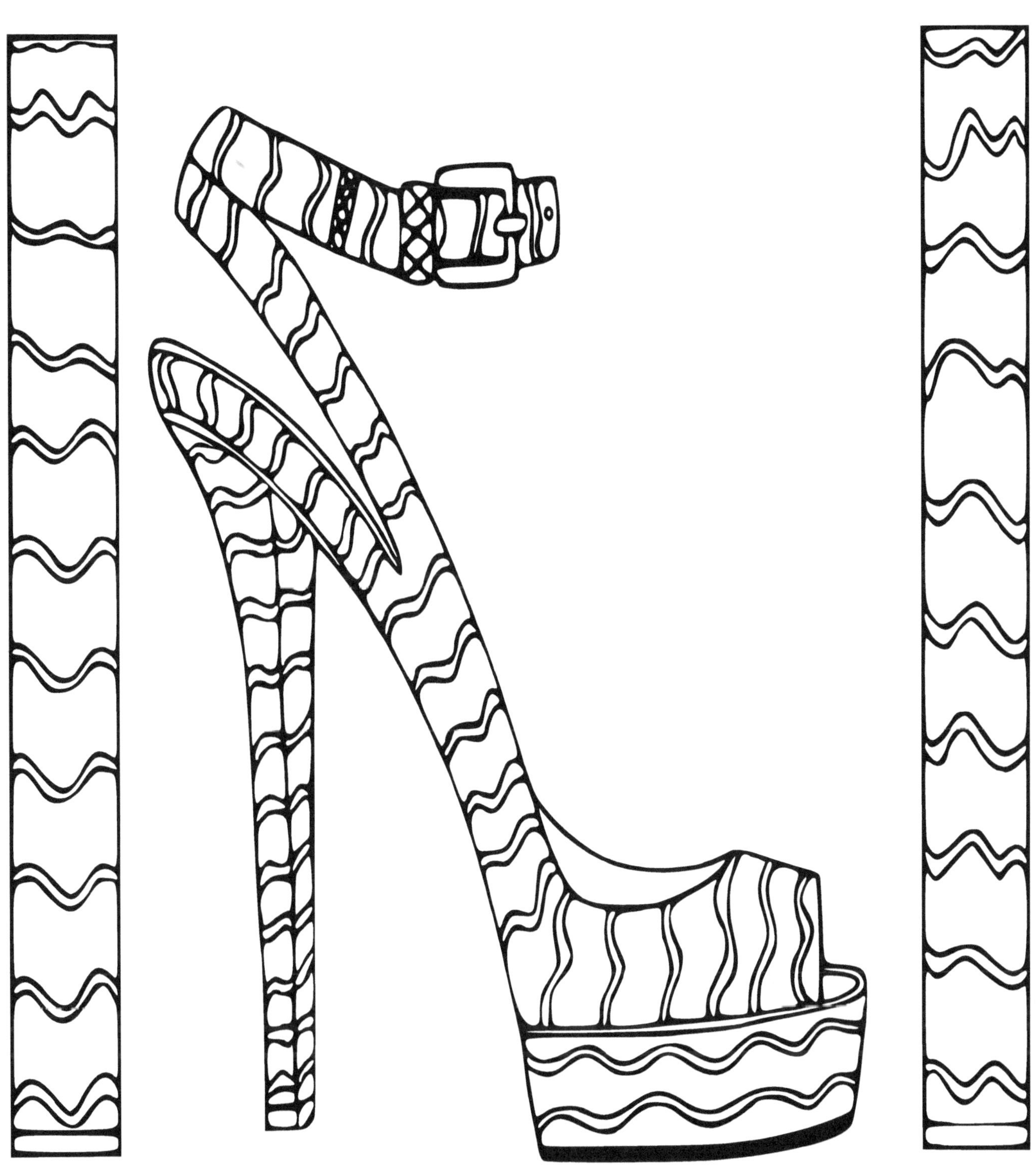

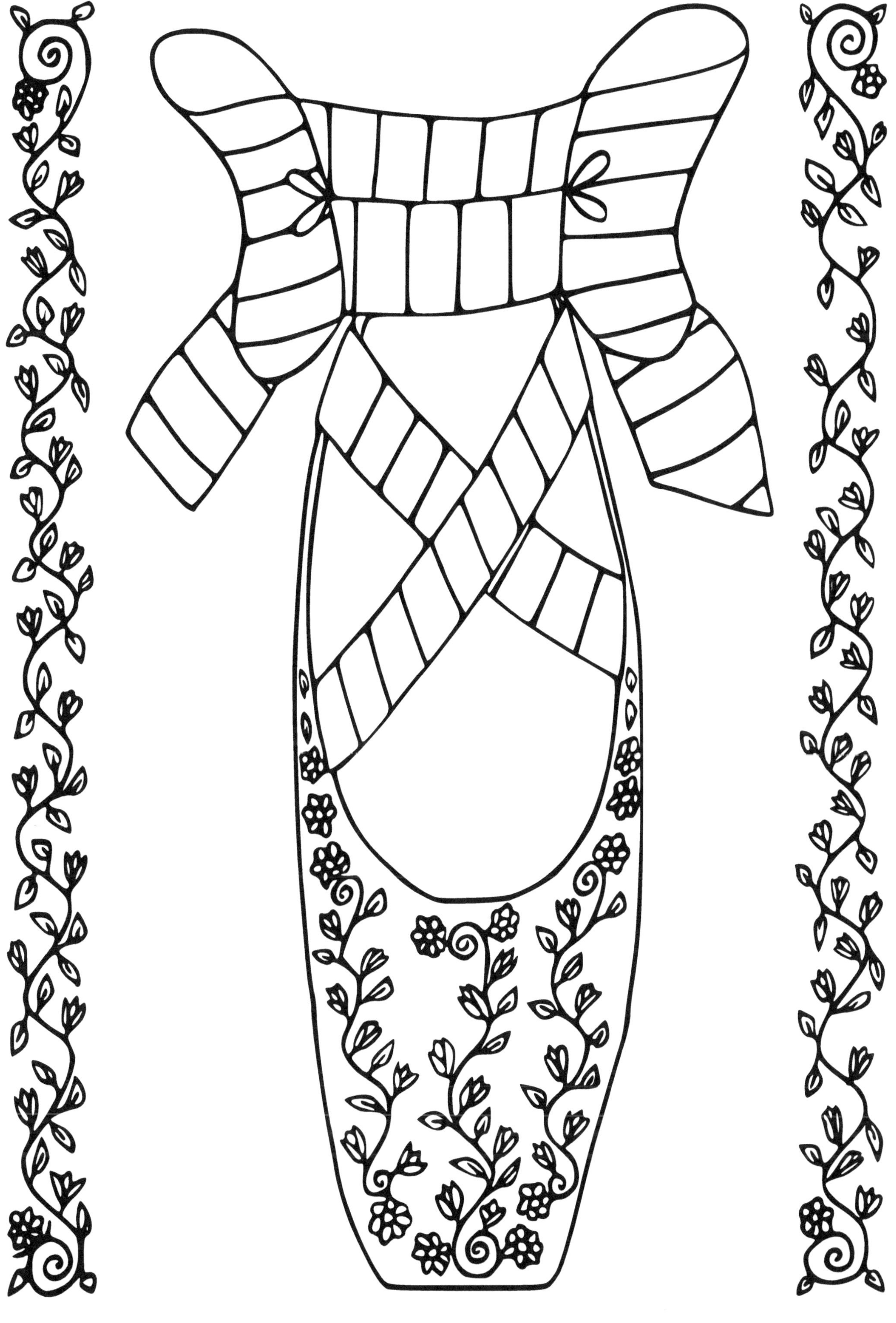

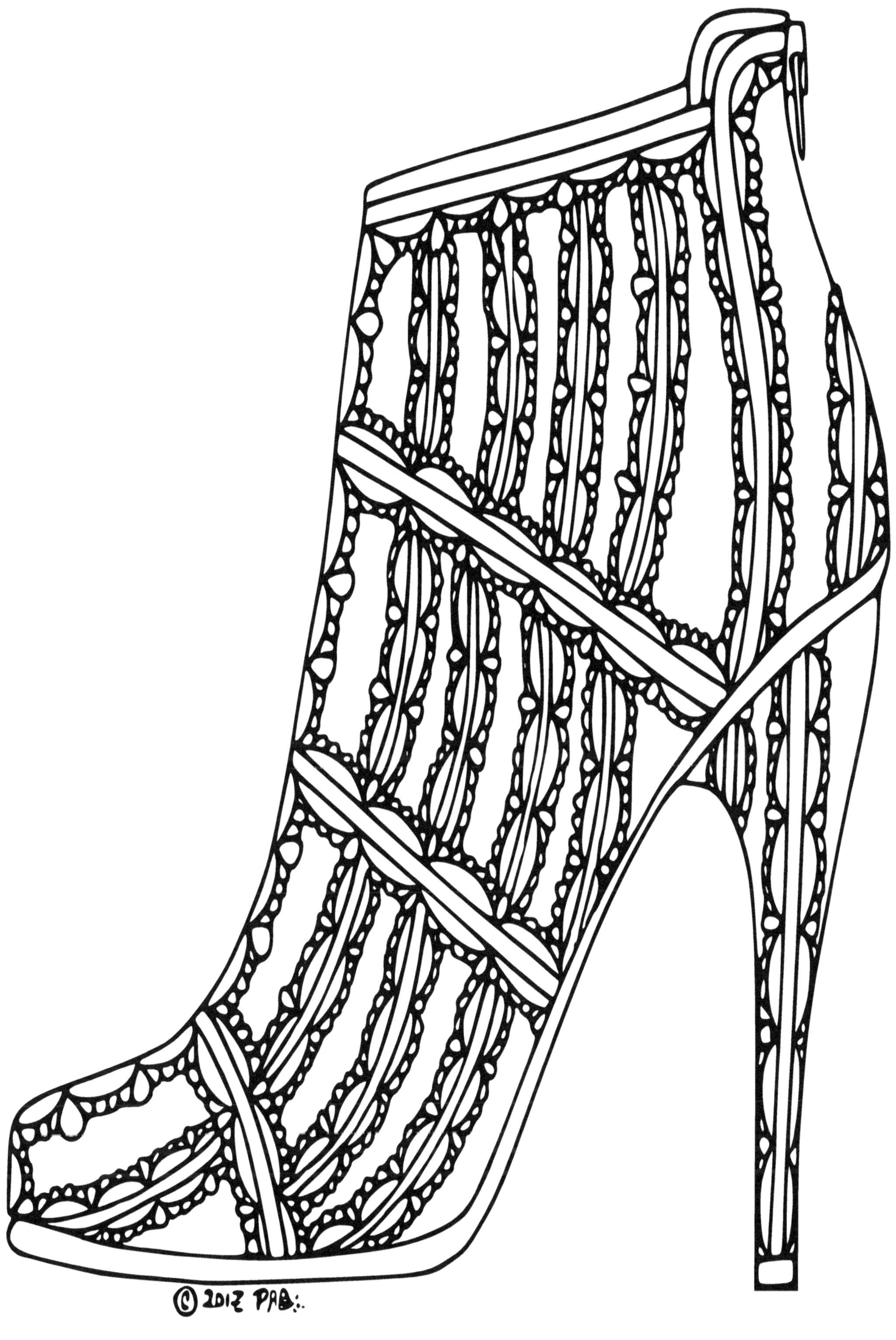
© 2012 PAB

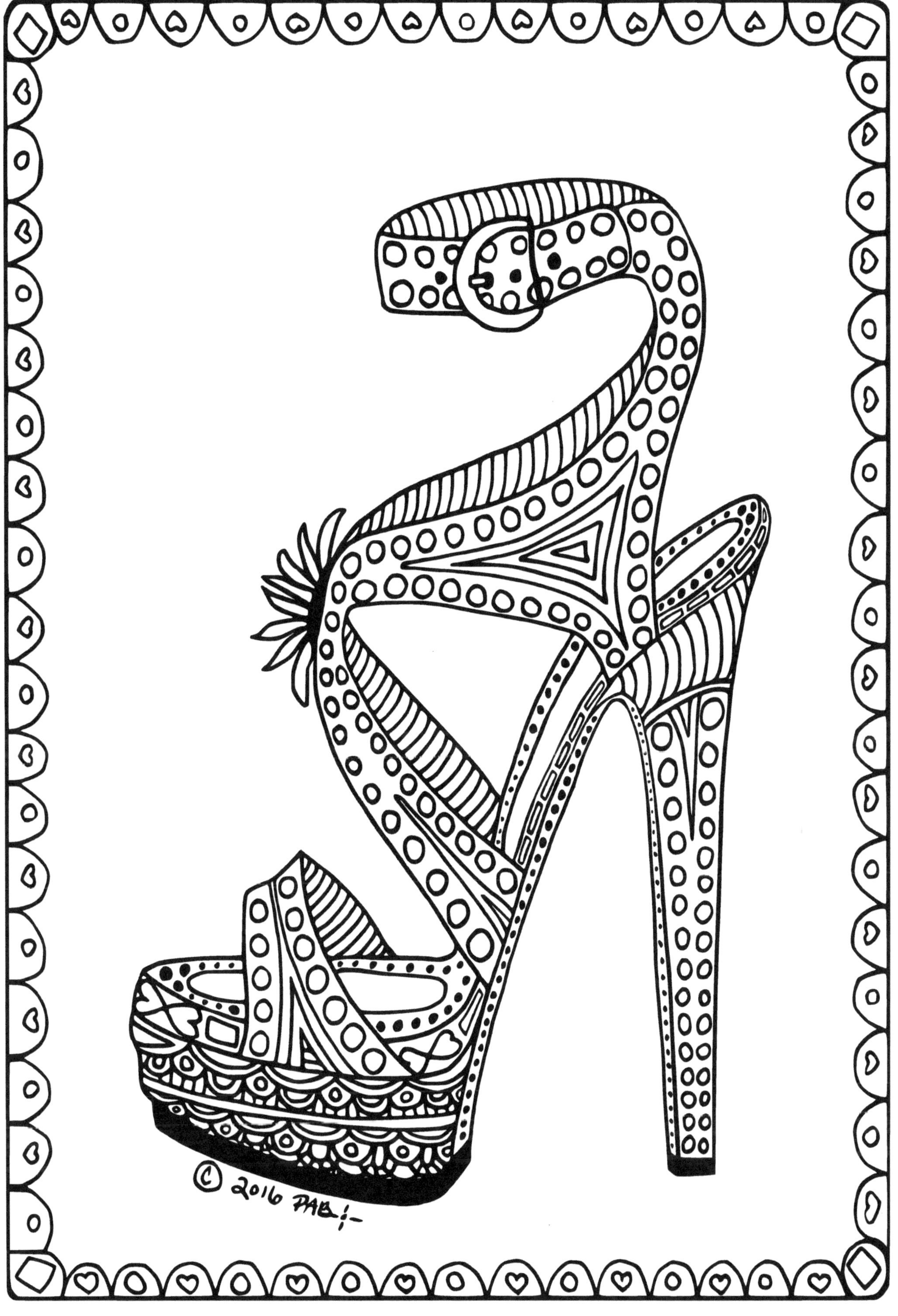
© 2016 PAB

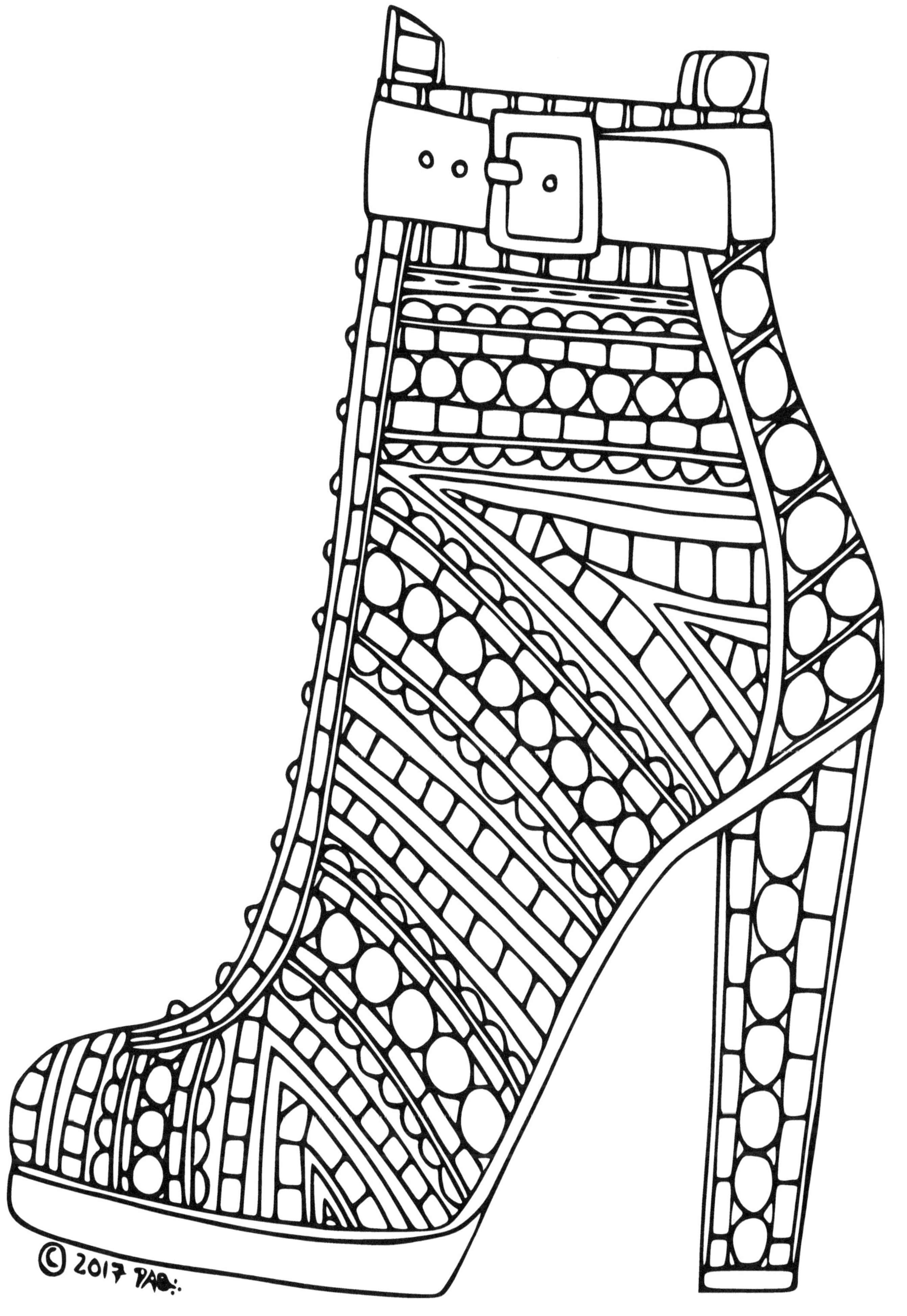
© 2017 PAB

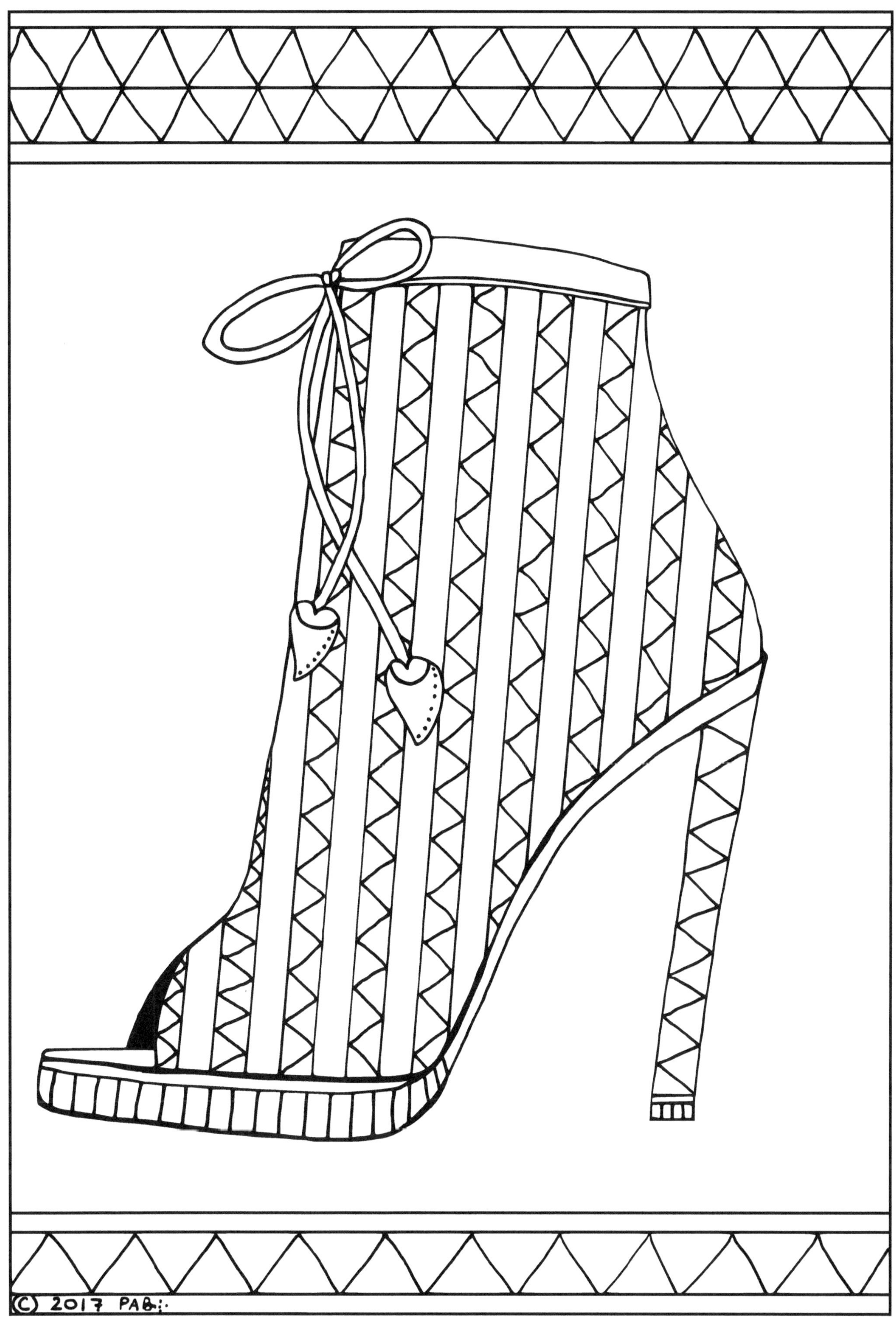
(C) 2017 PAB

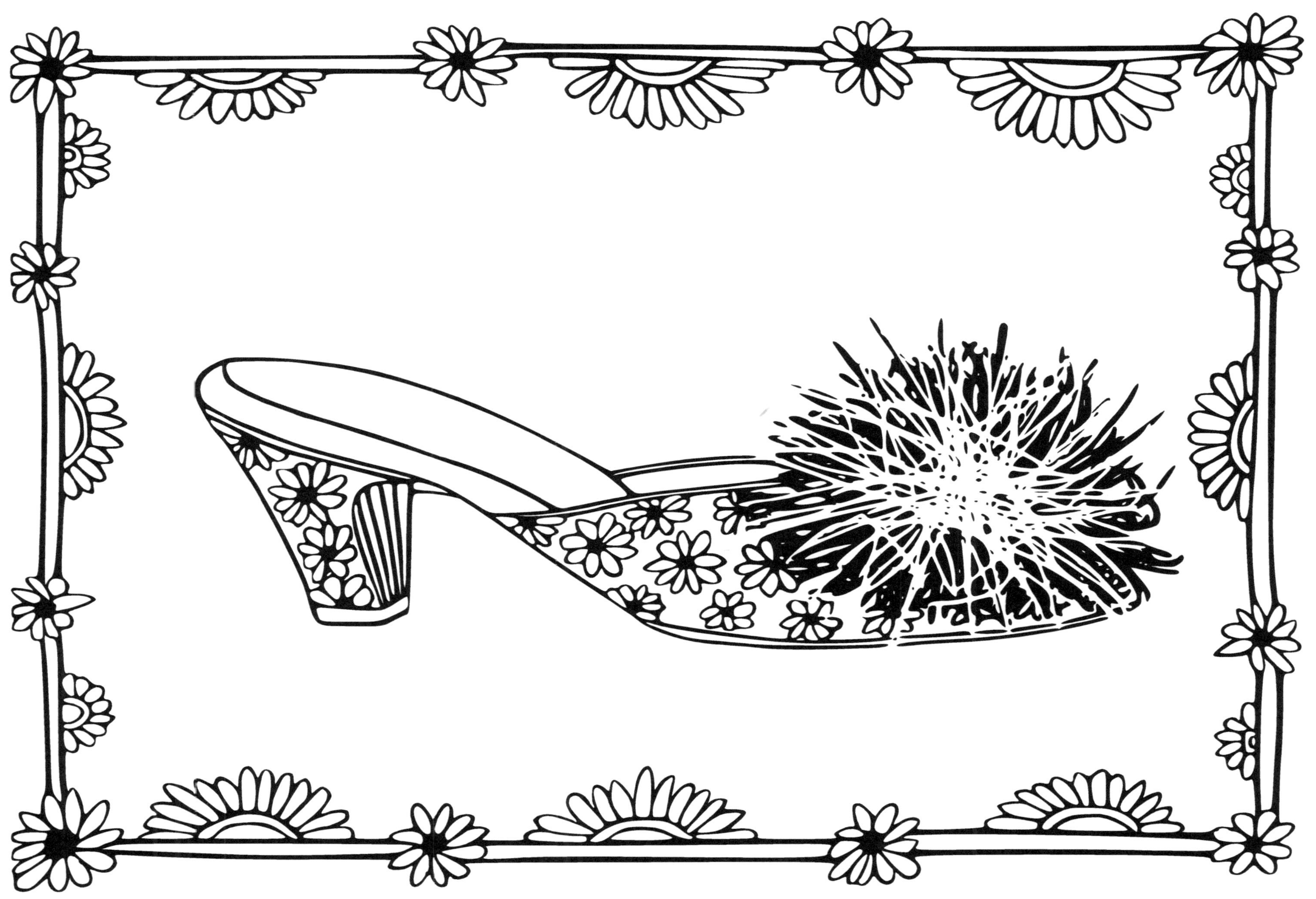

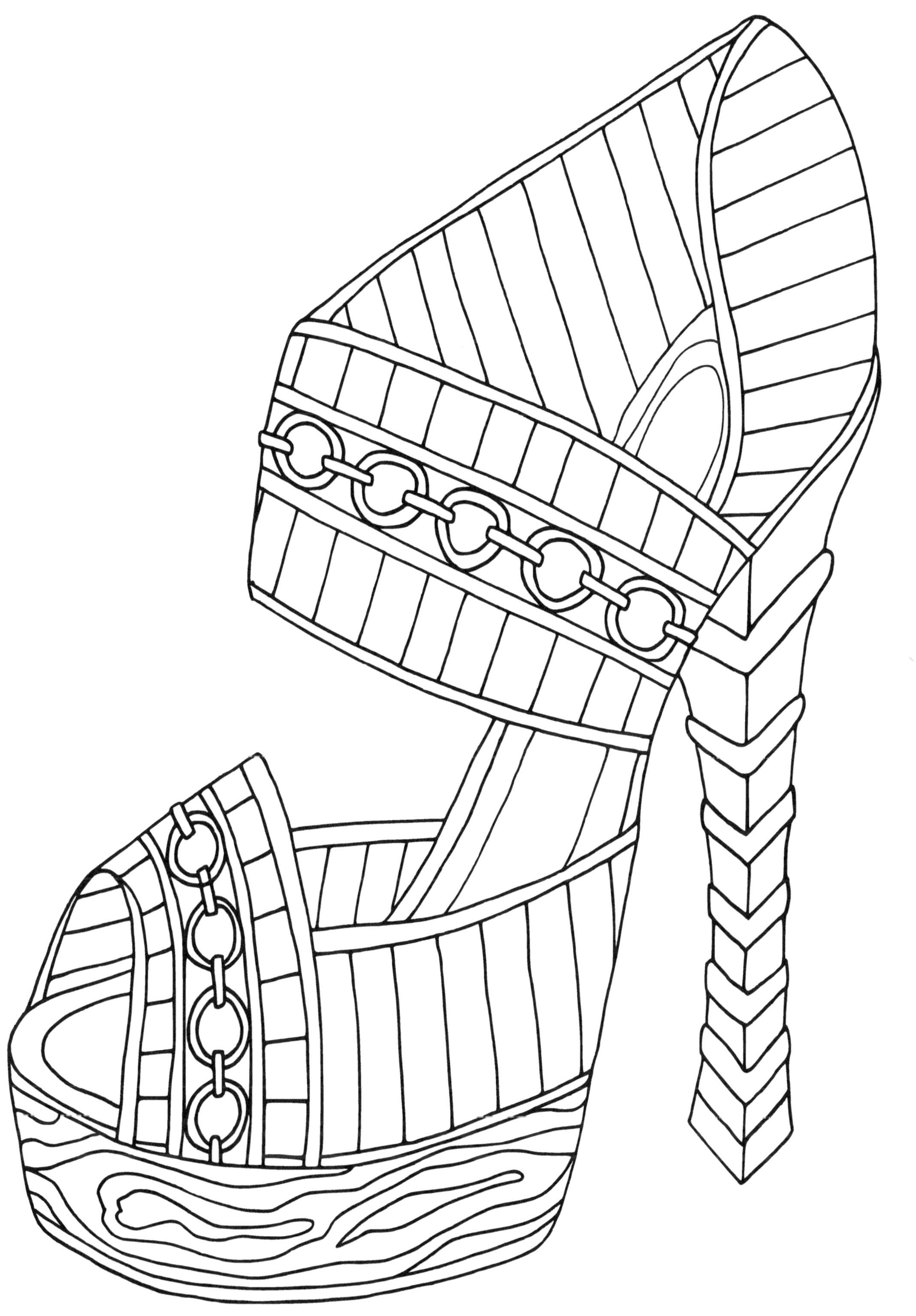

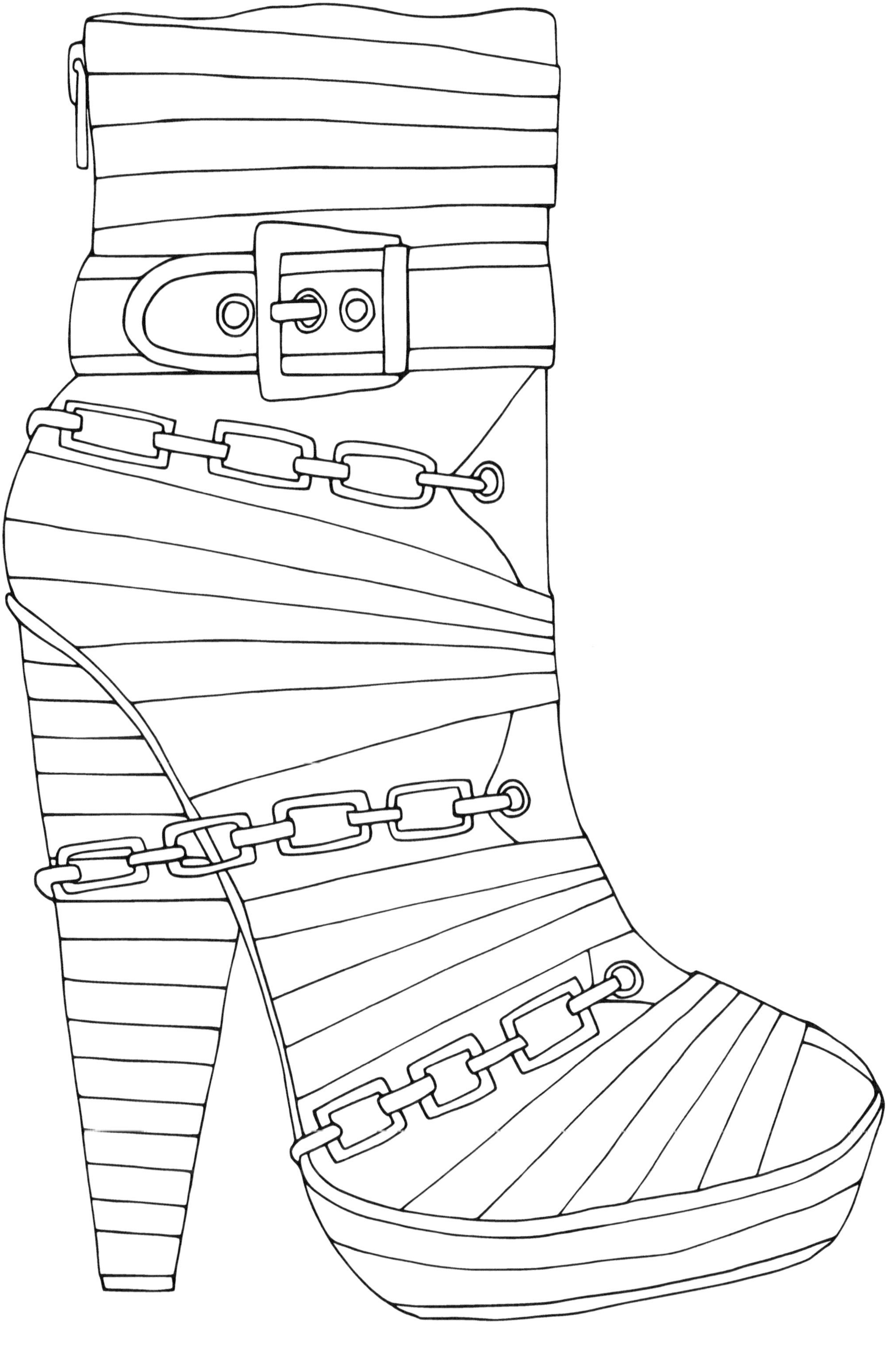

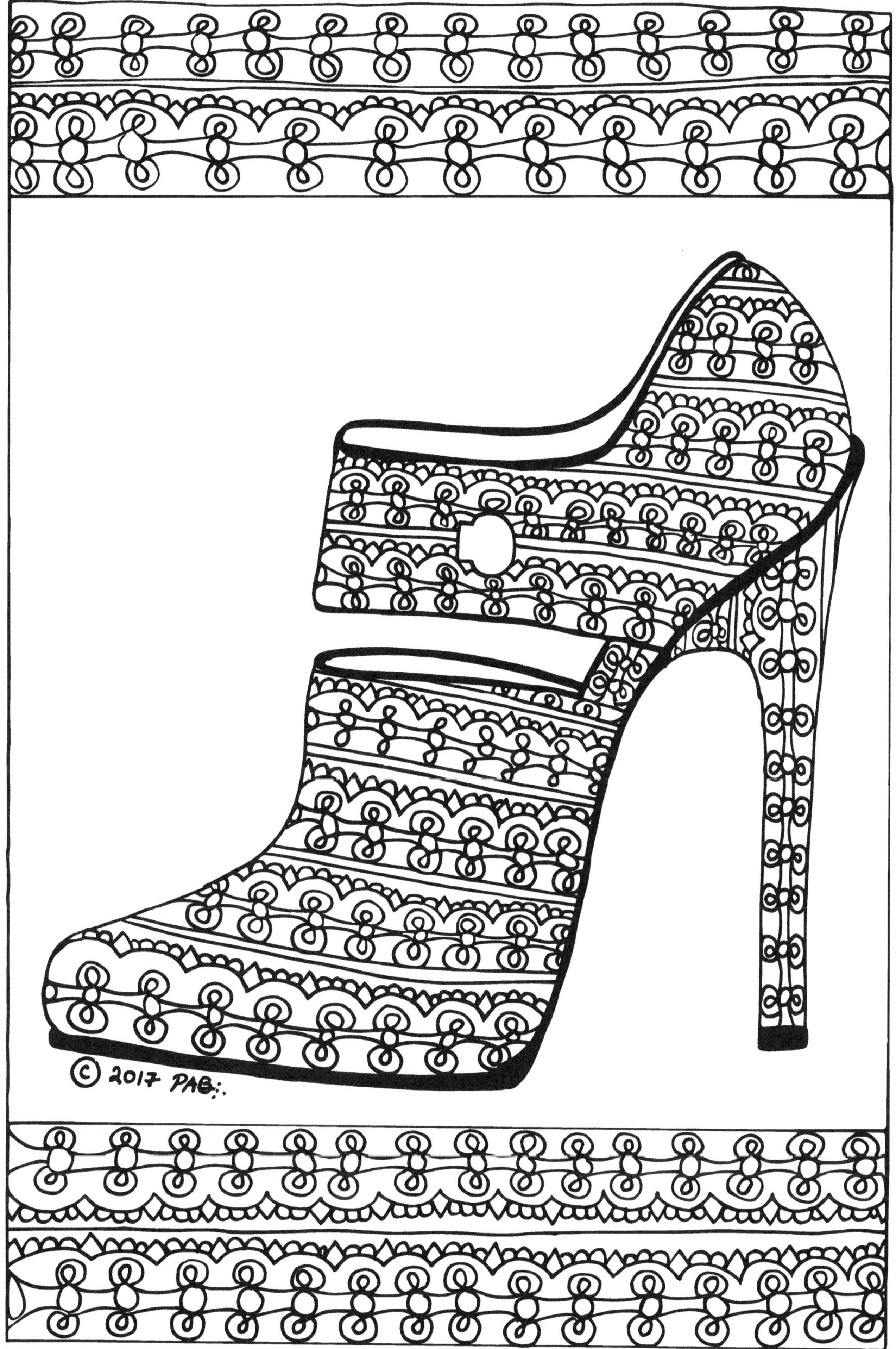
© 2017 PAB

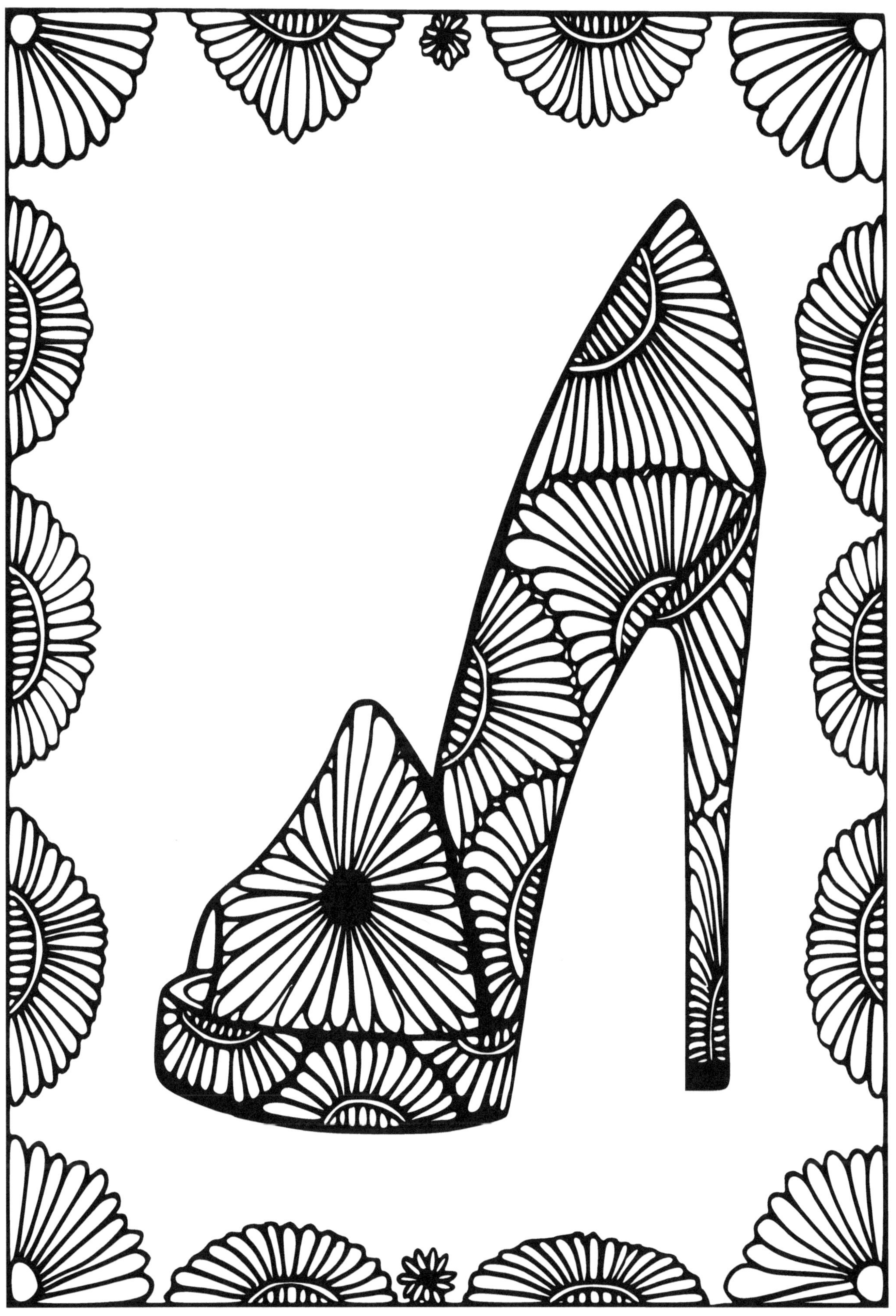

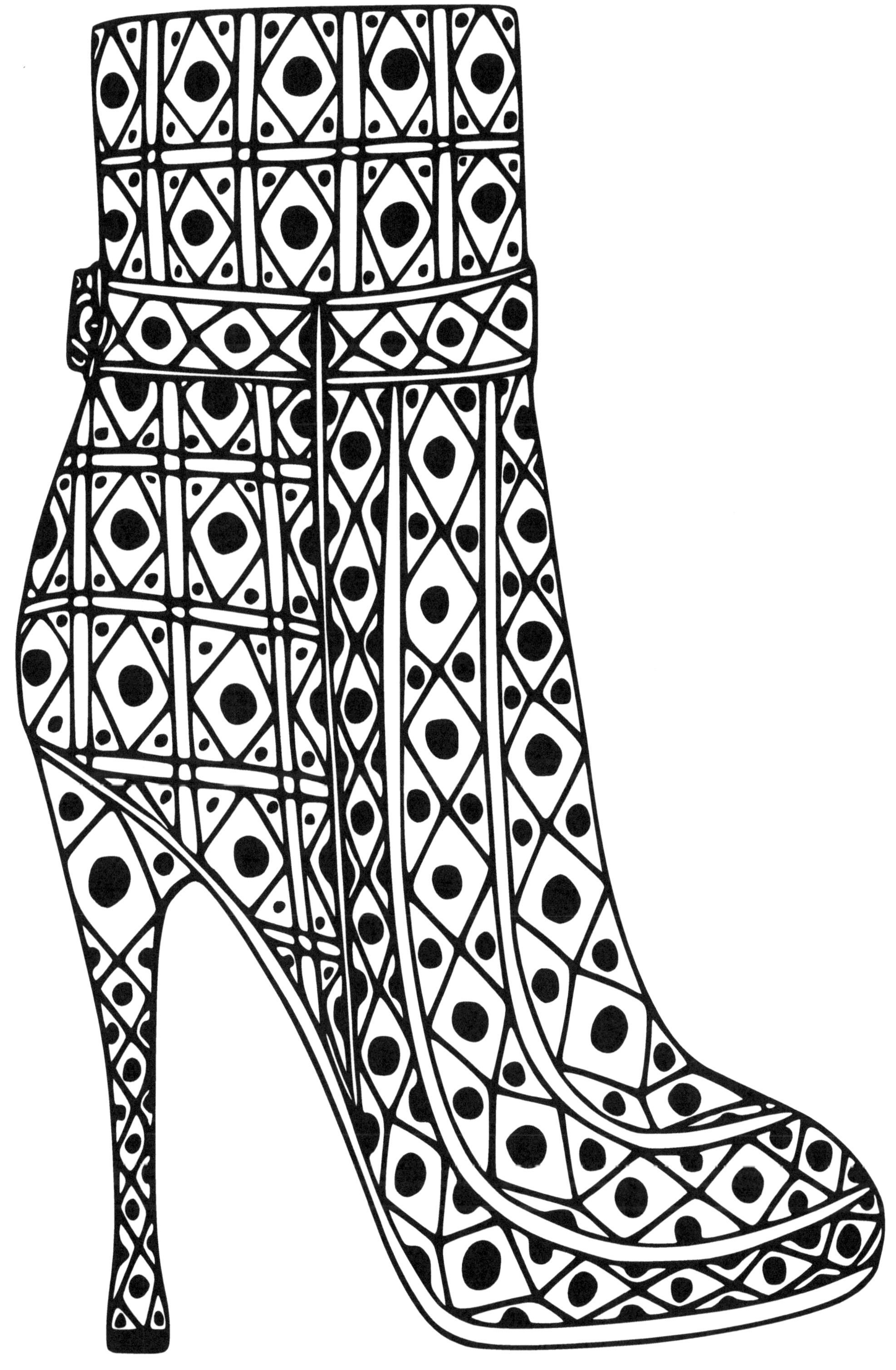

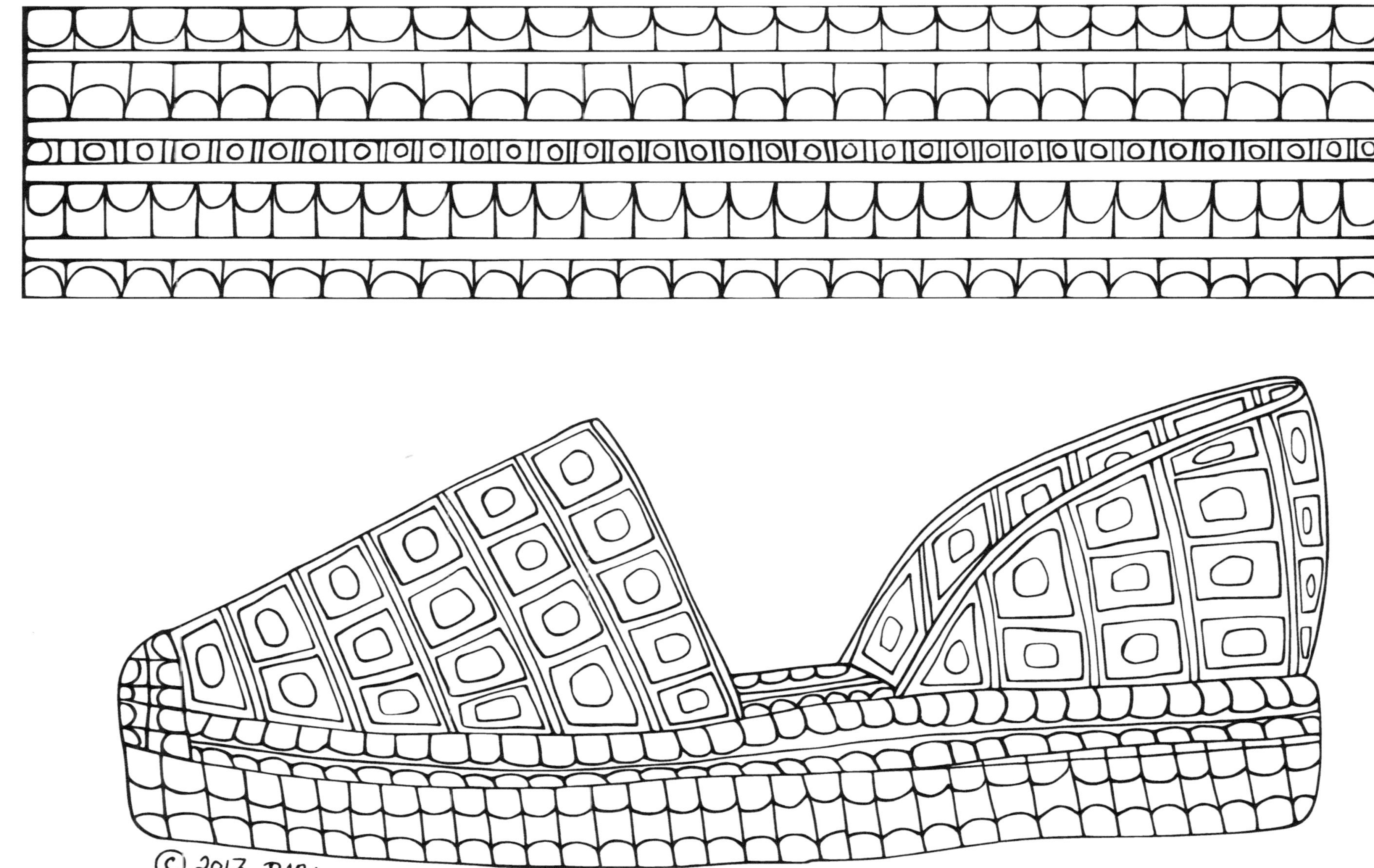
© 2017 PAB

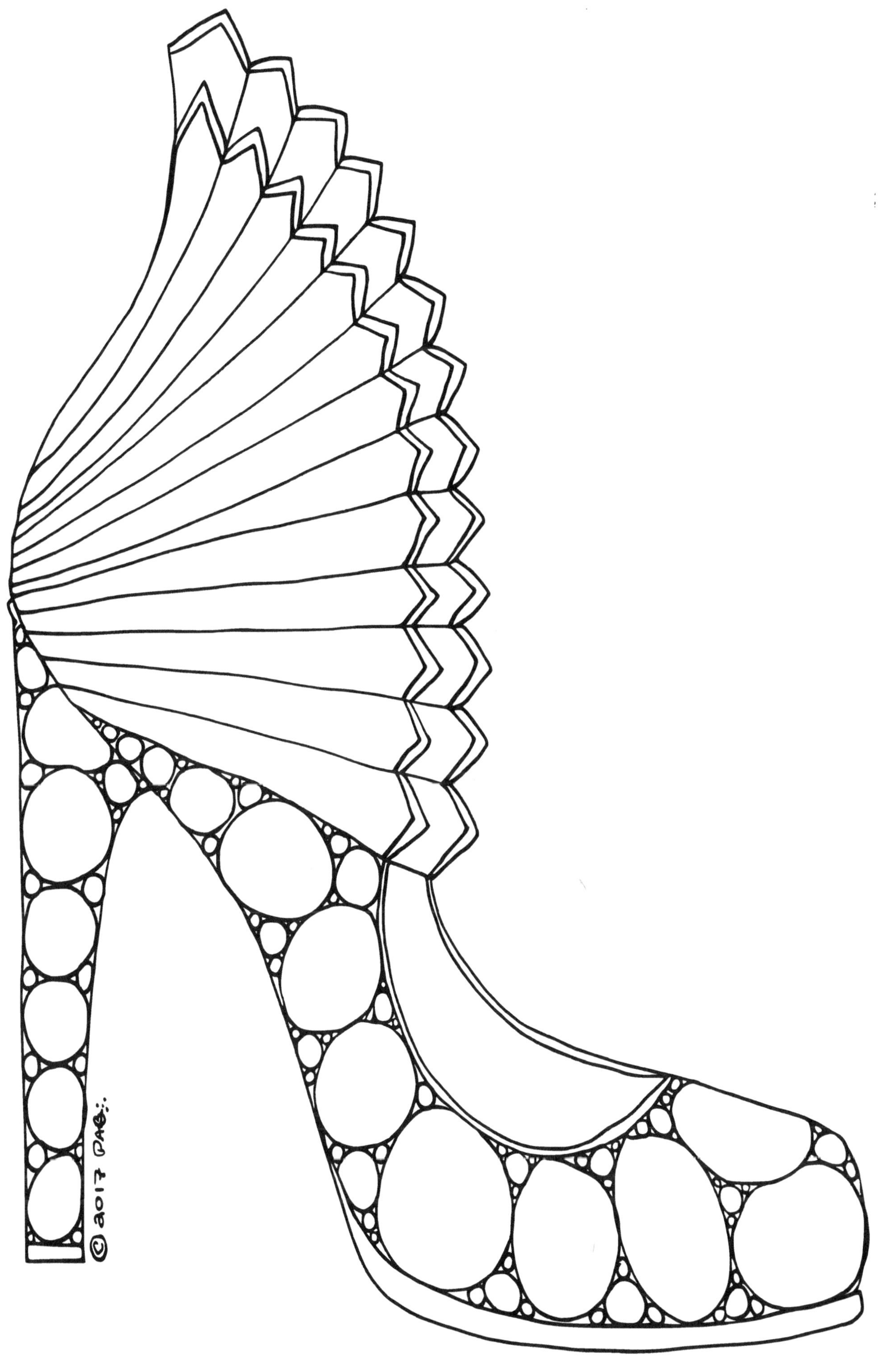
© 2017 PAB

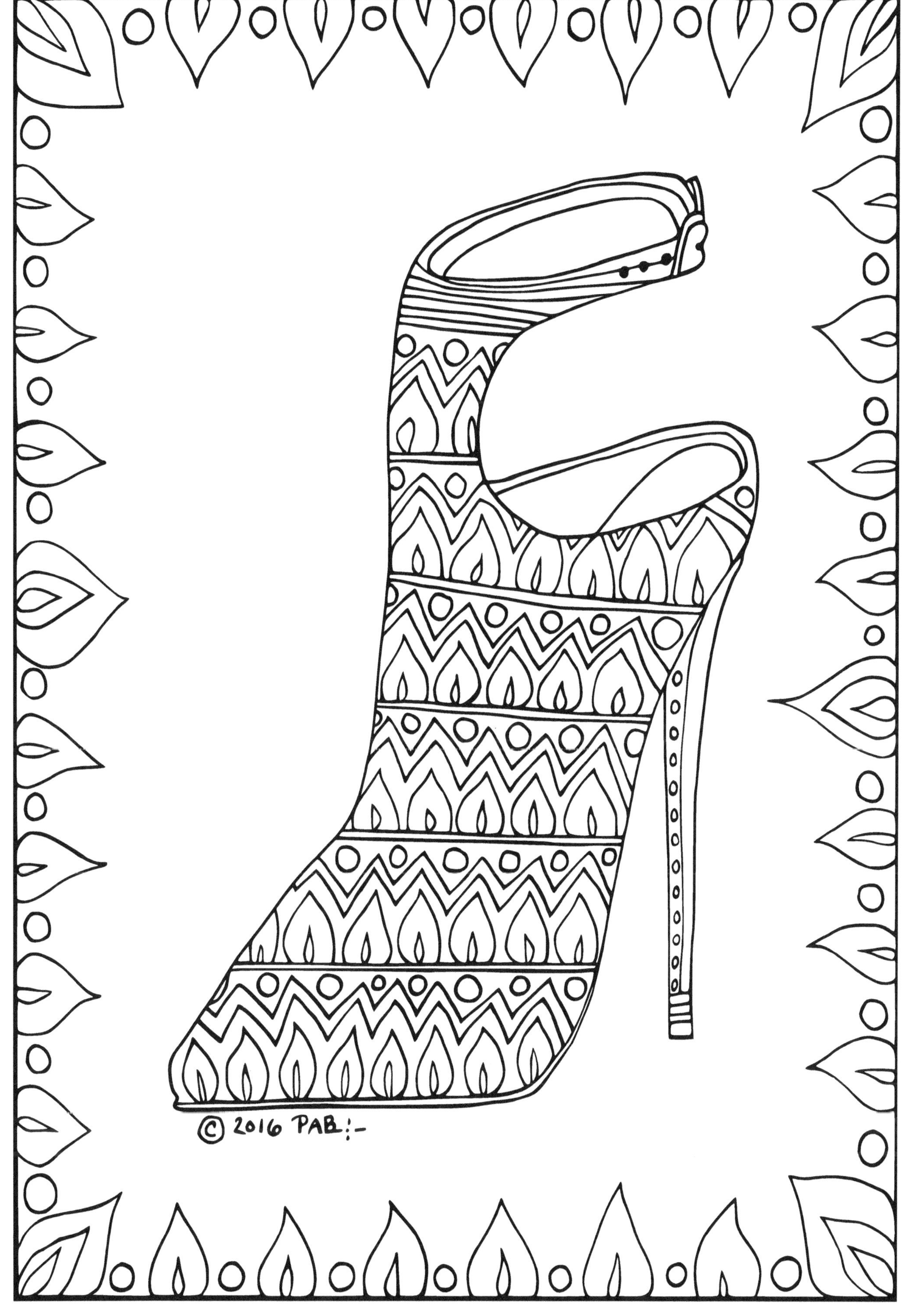
© 2016 PAB :-

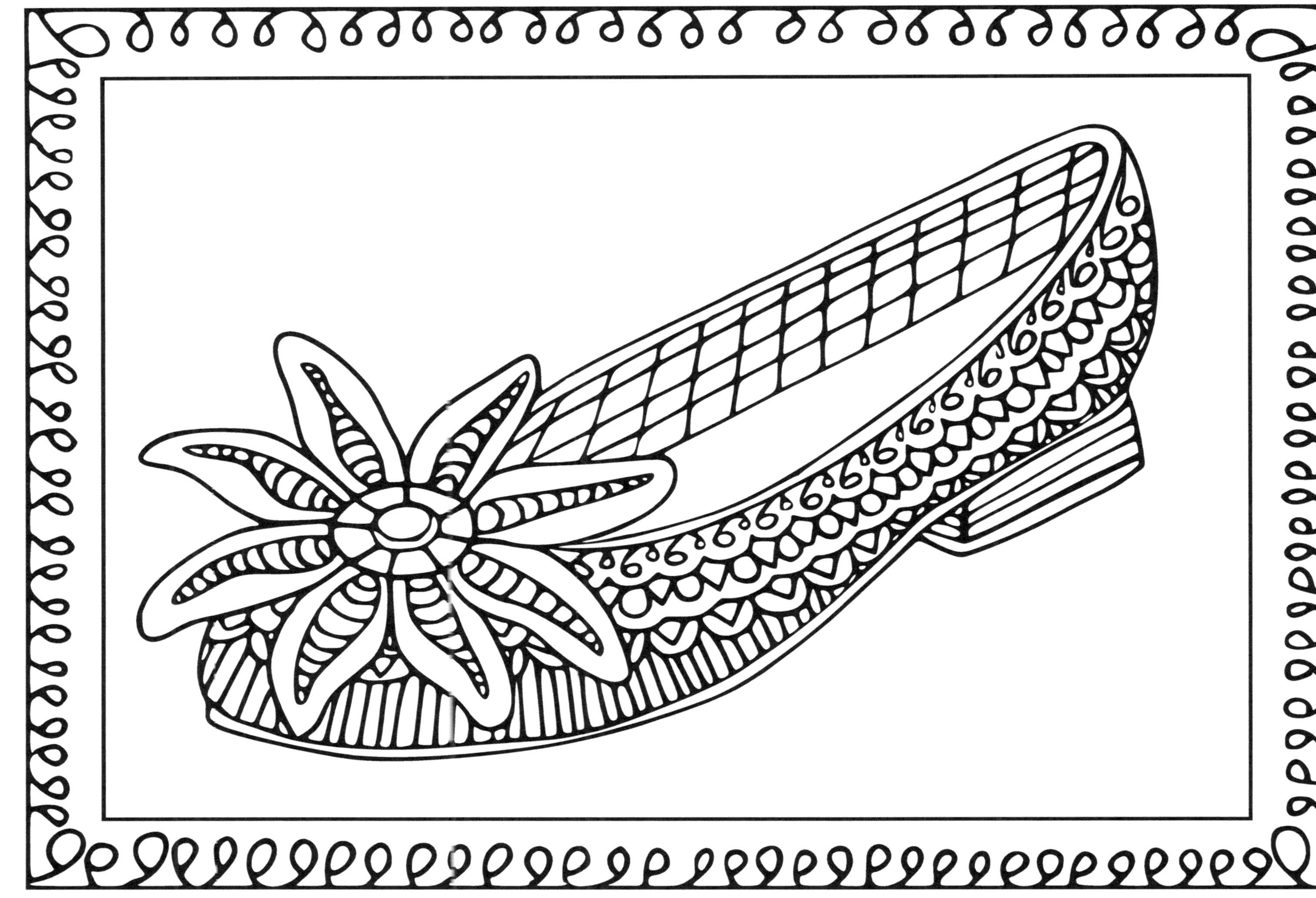

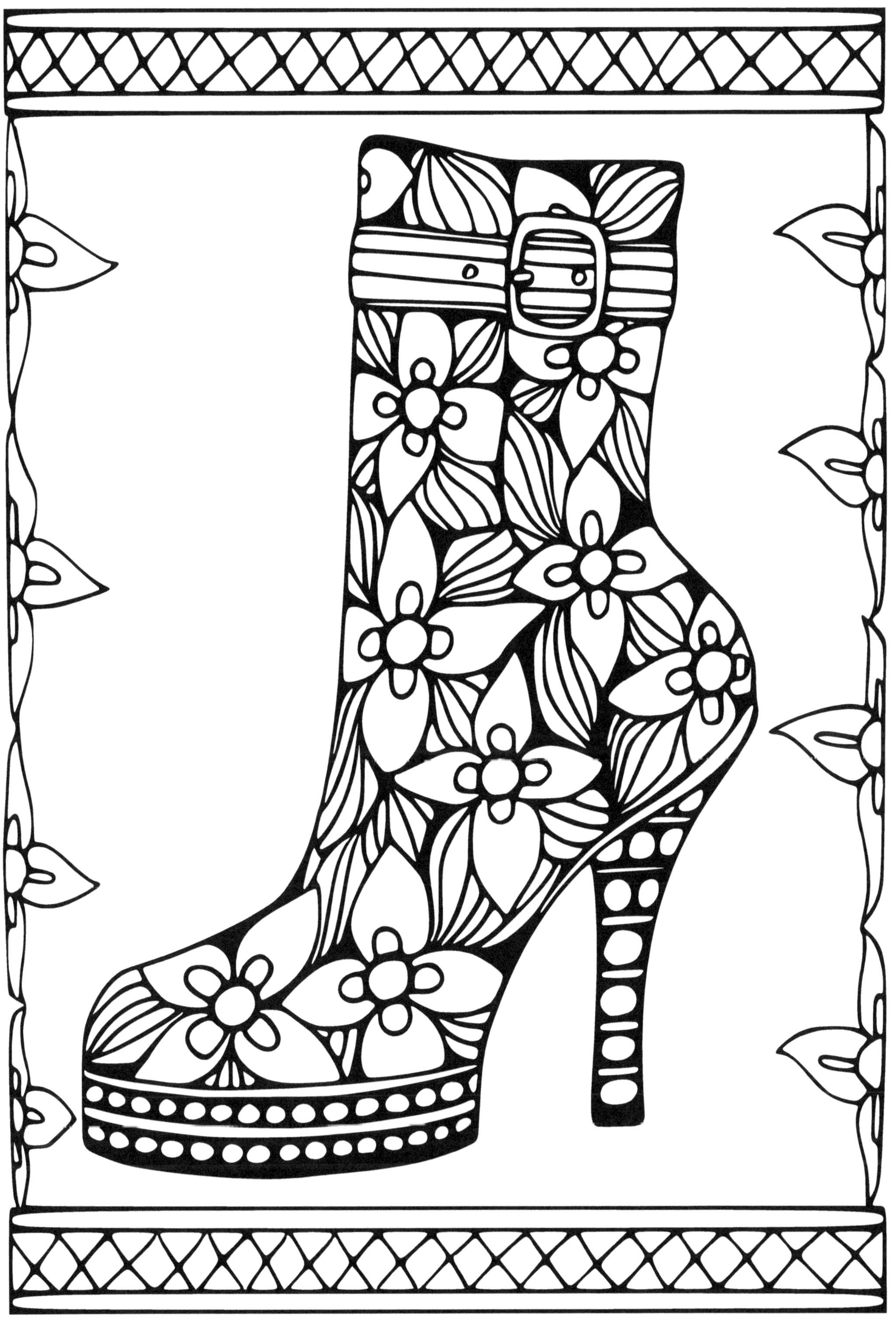

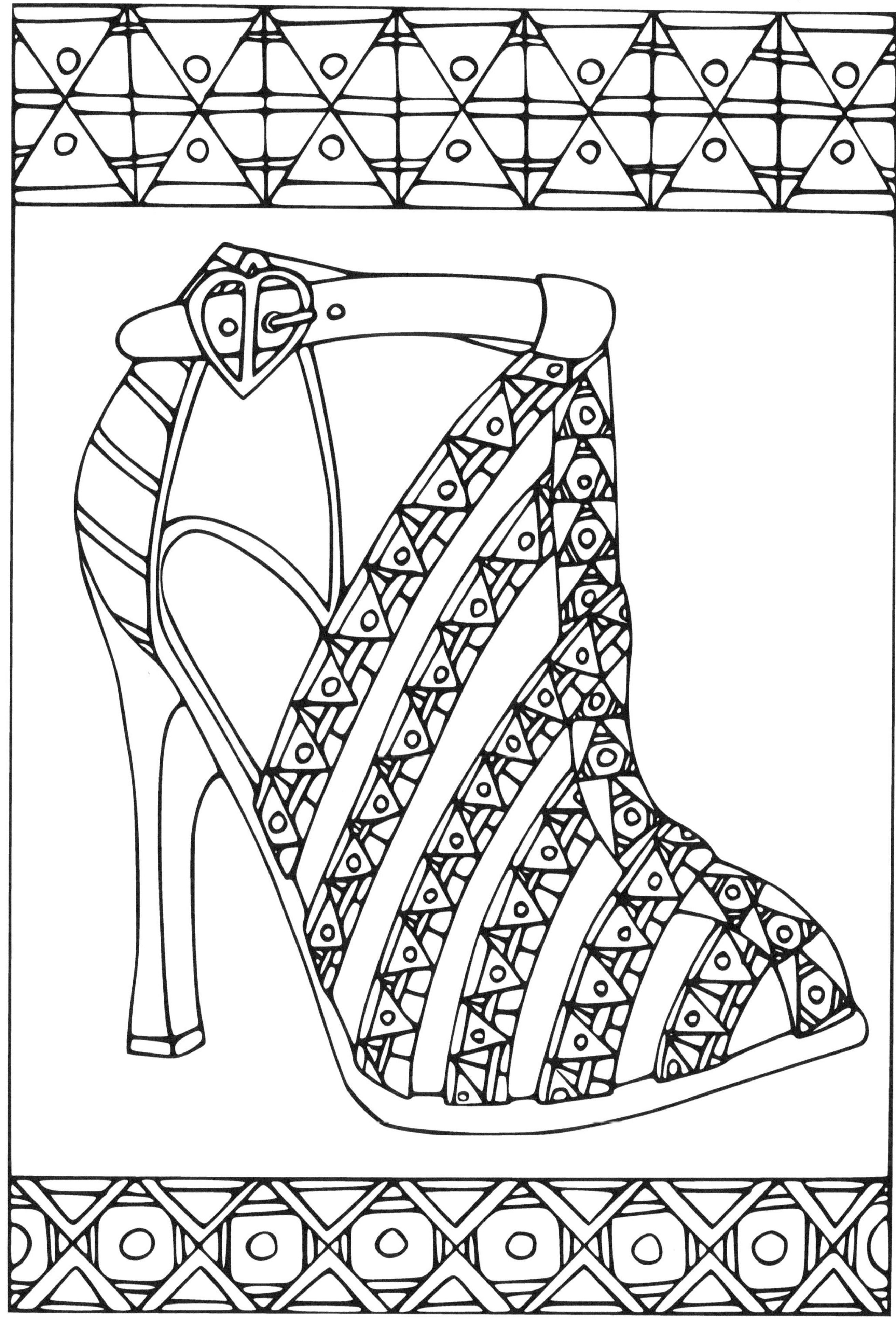

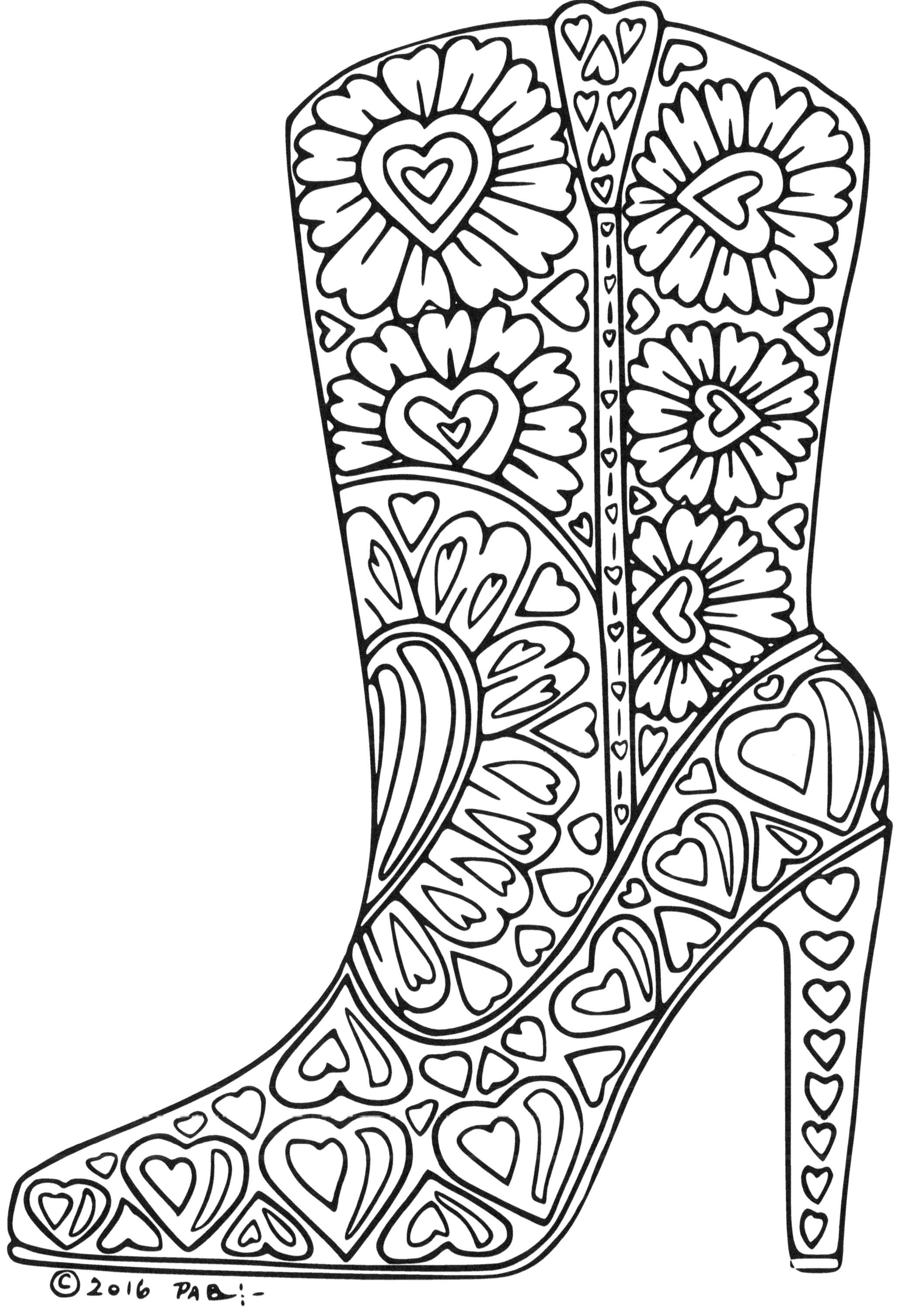

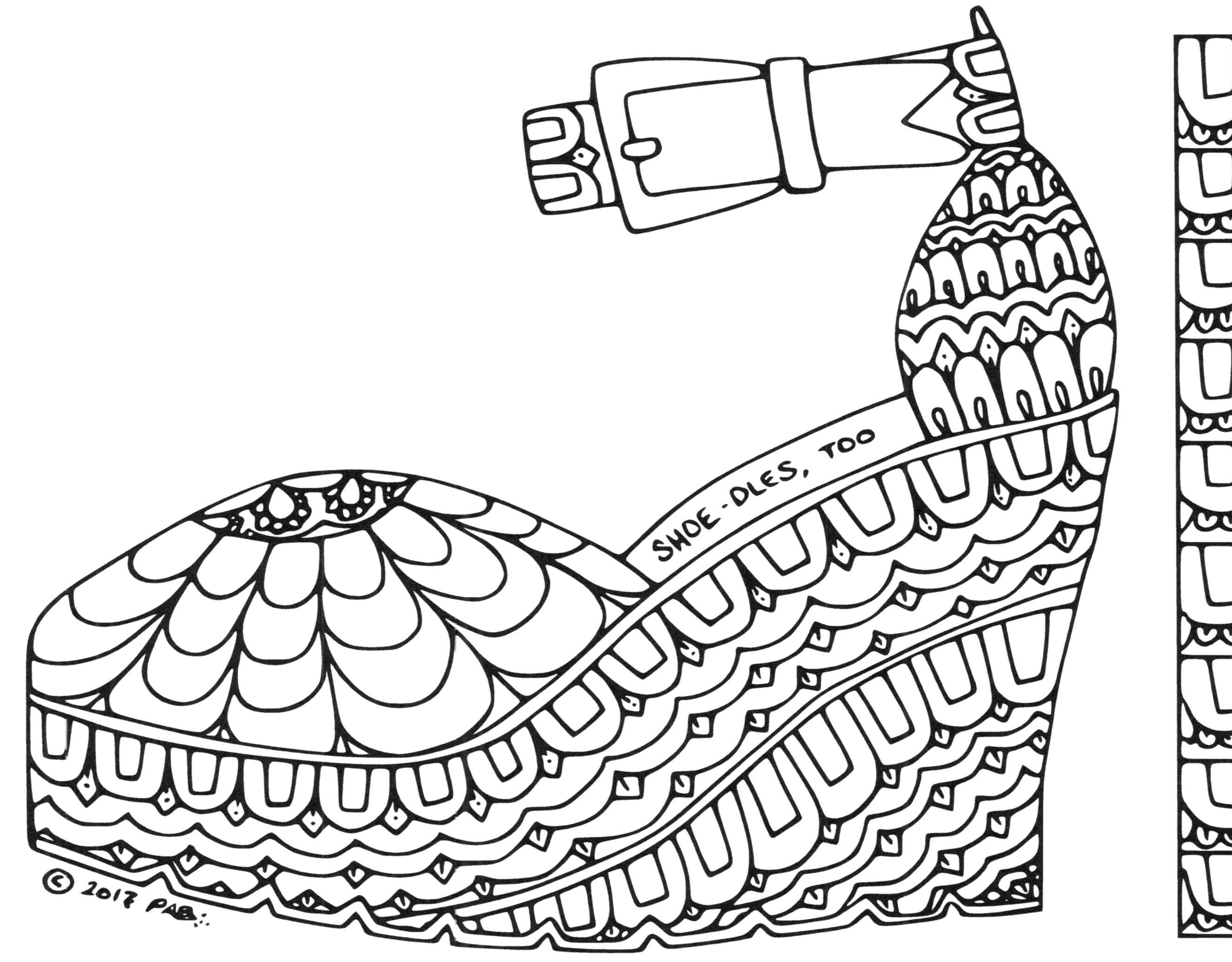
SHOE-DLES, TOO
© 2017 PAB

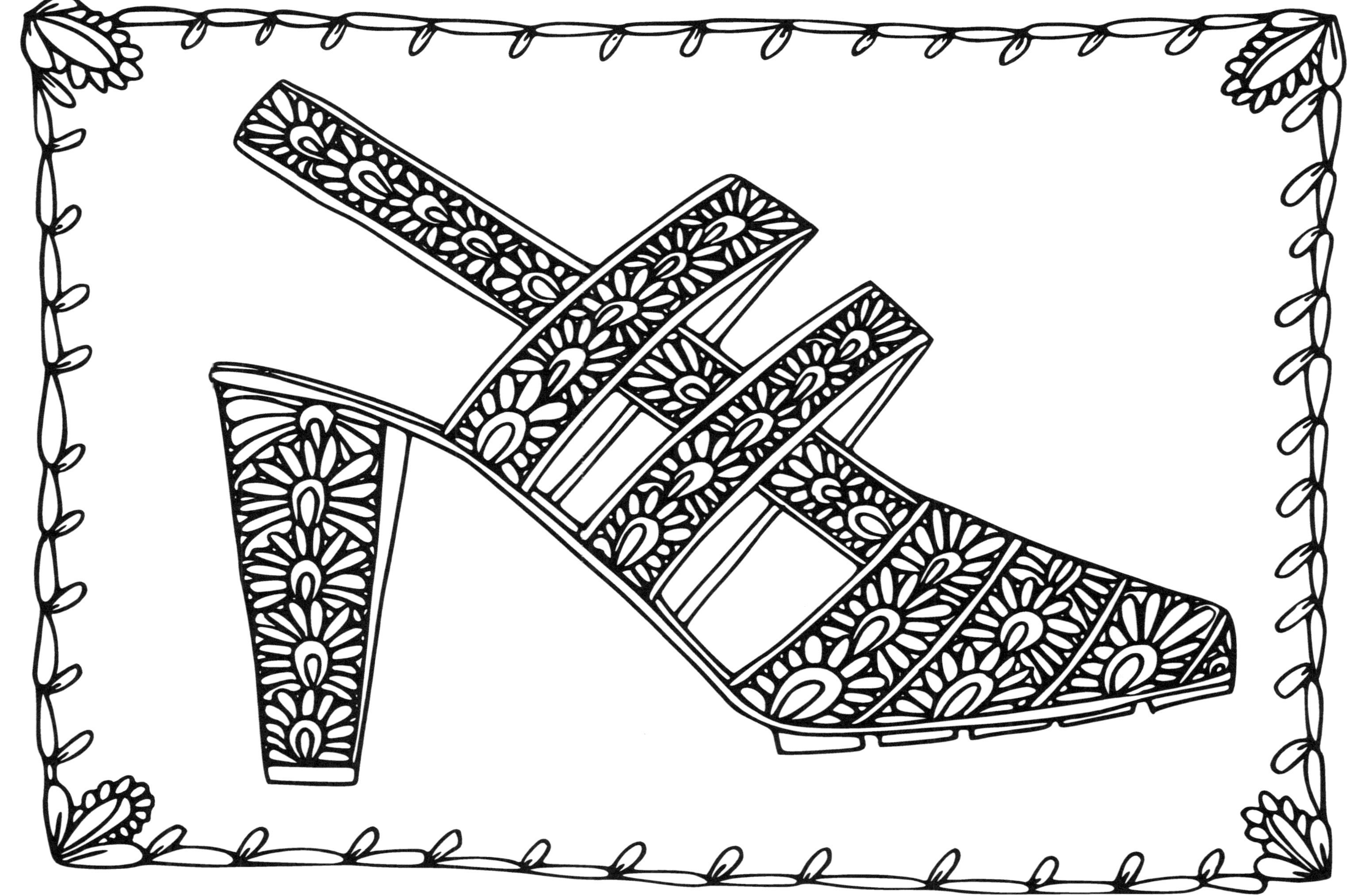

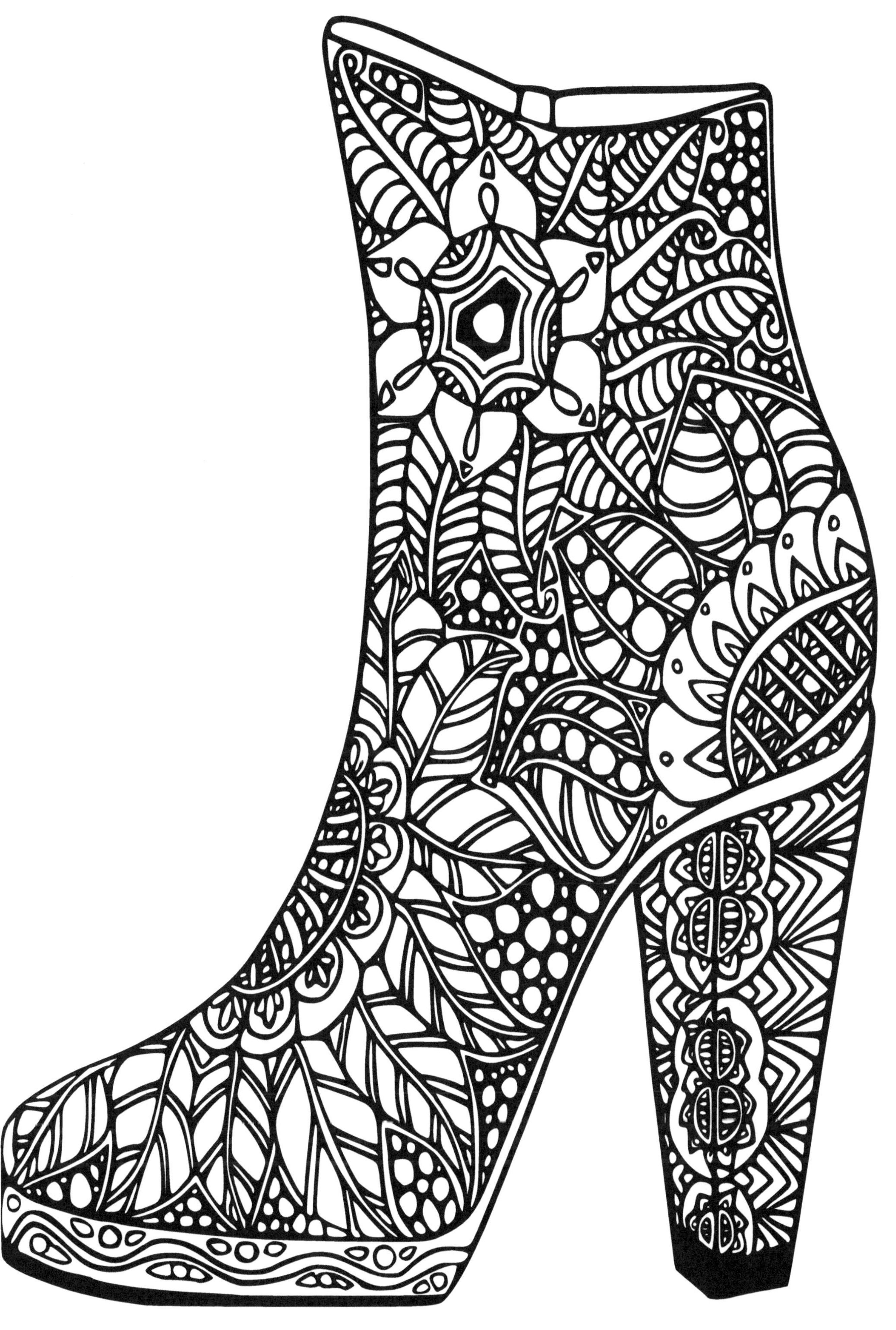

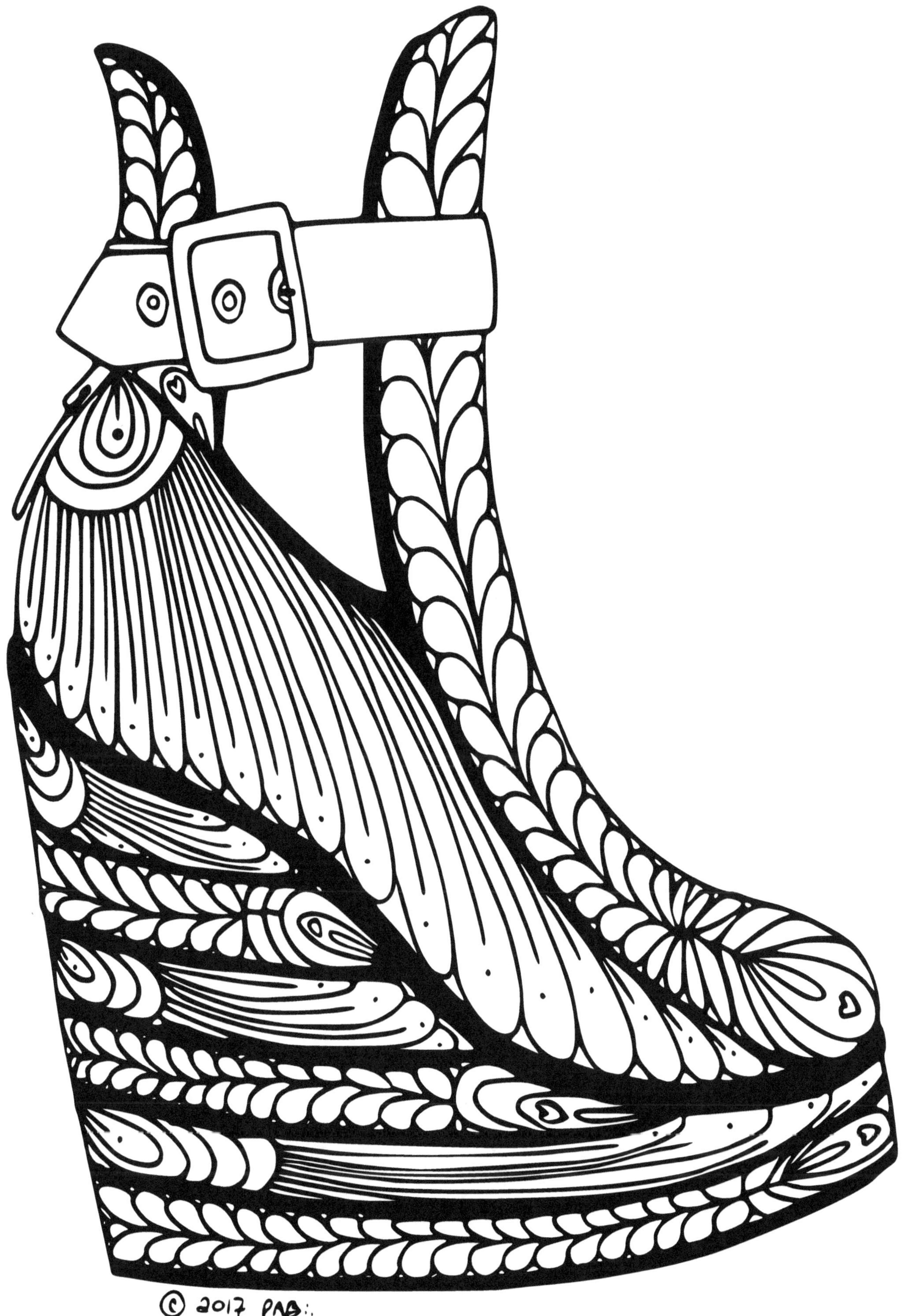
© 2017 PAB

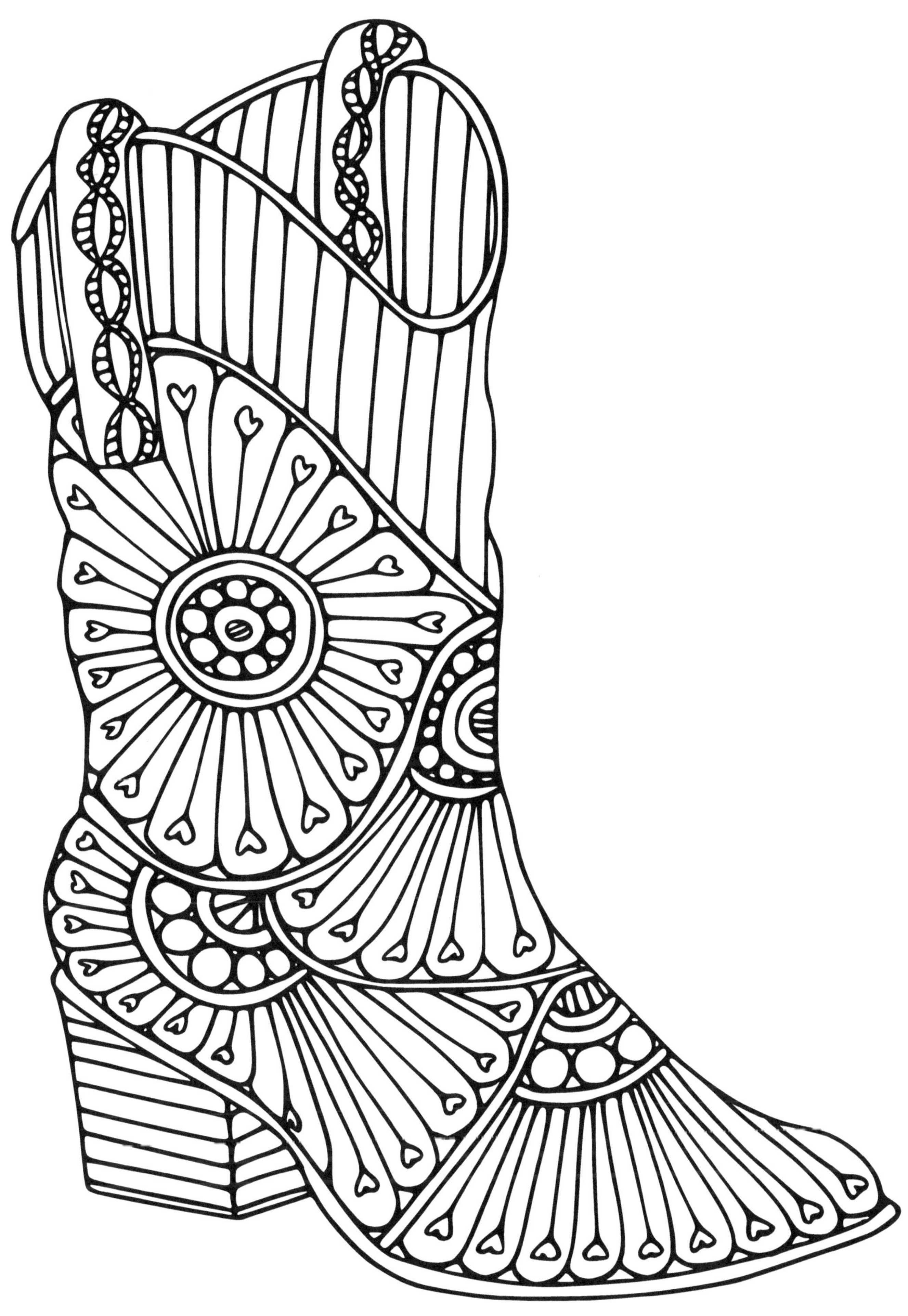

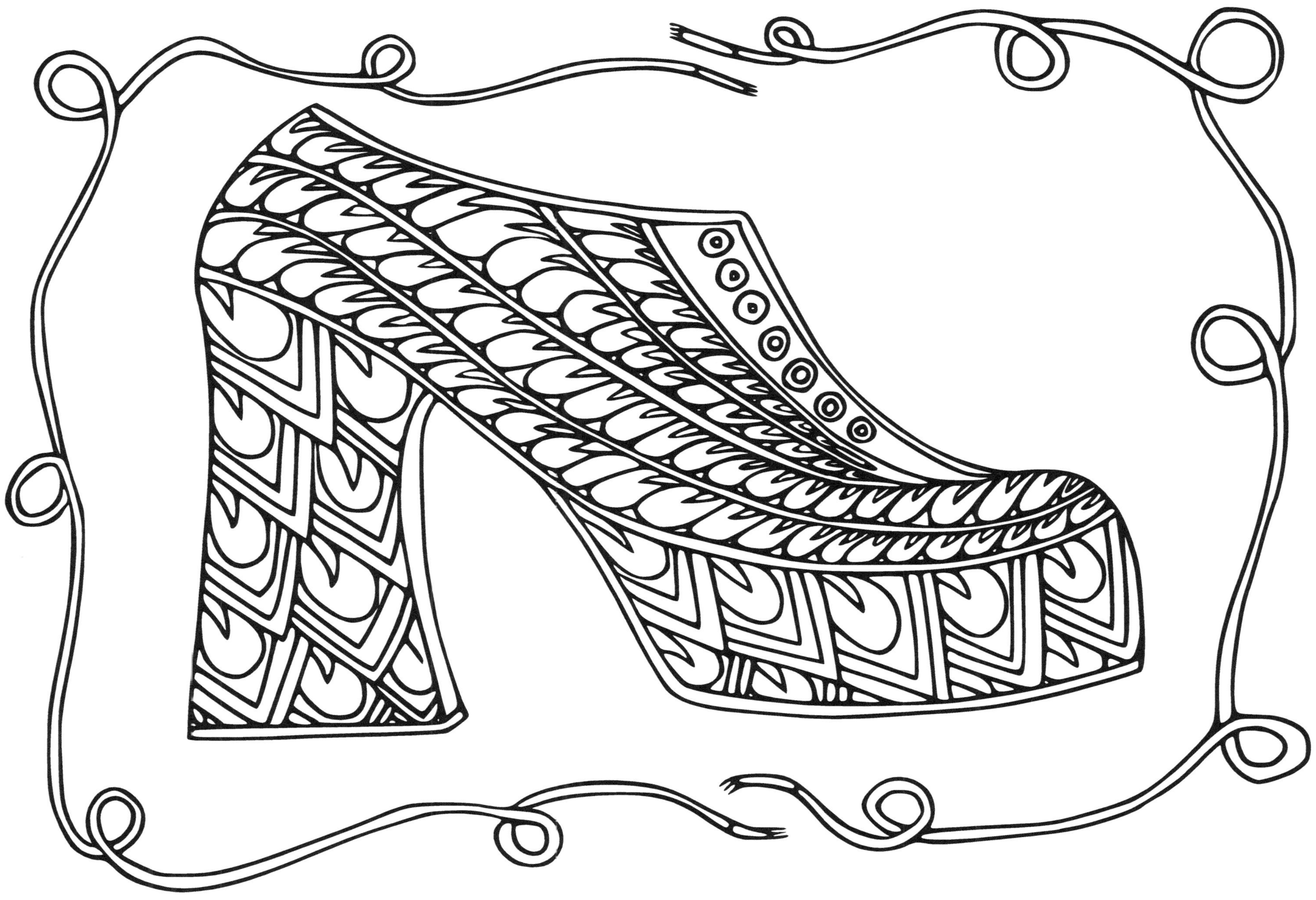

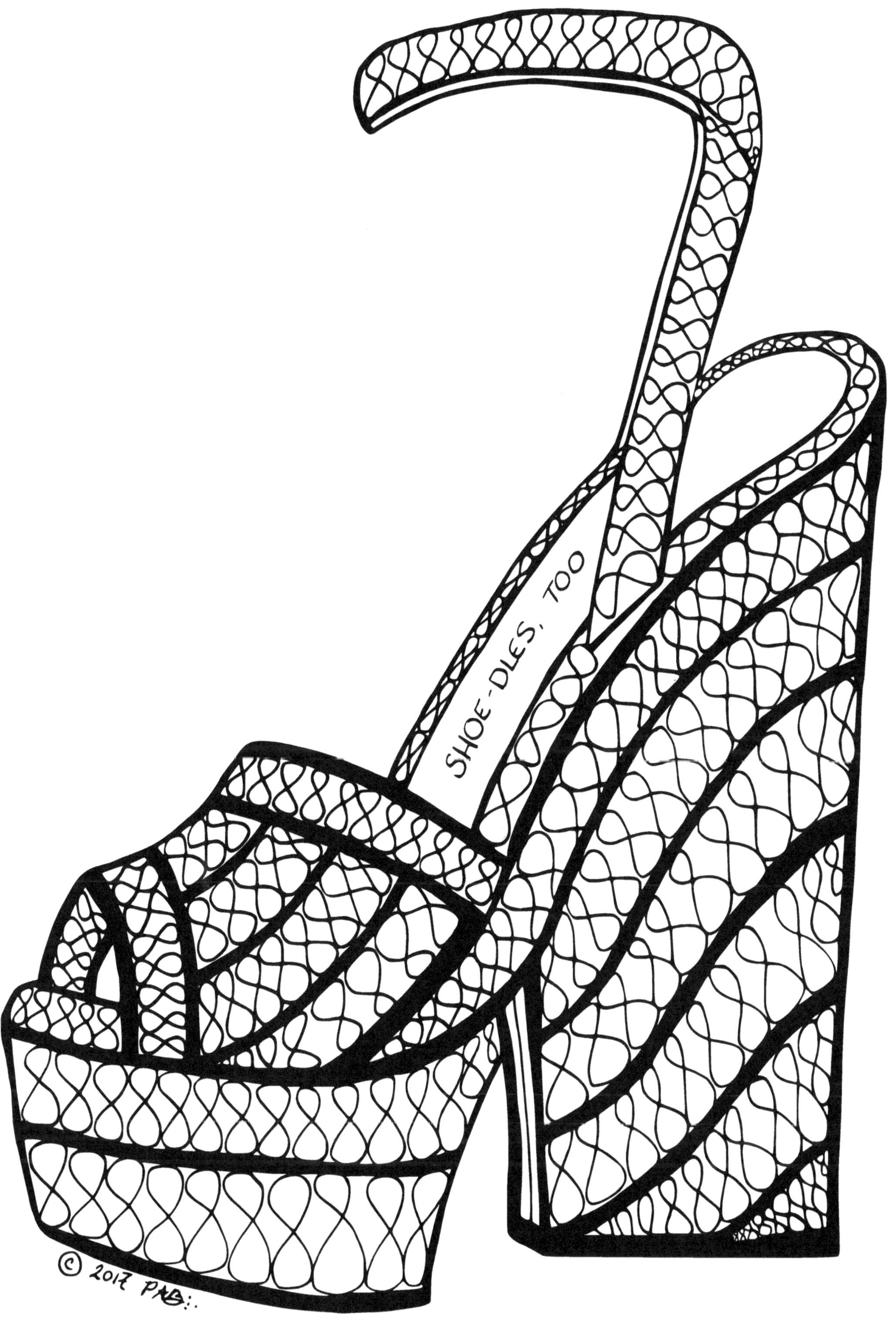
SHOE-DLES, TOO
© 2017 PAB

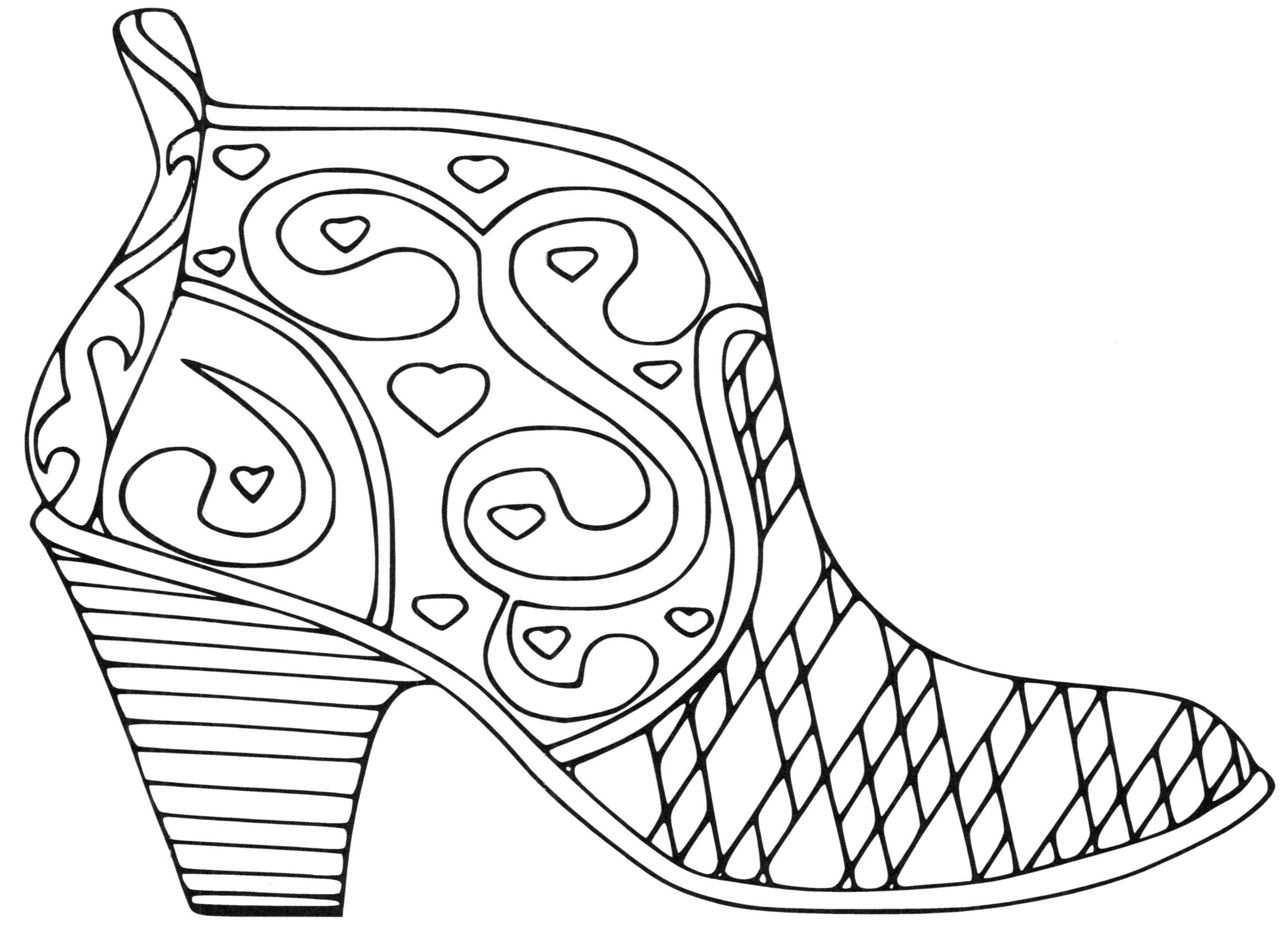

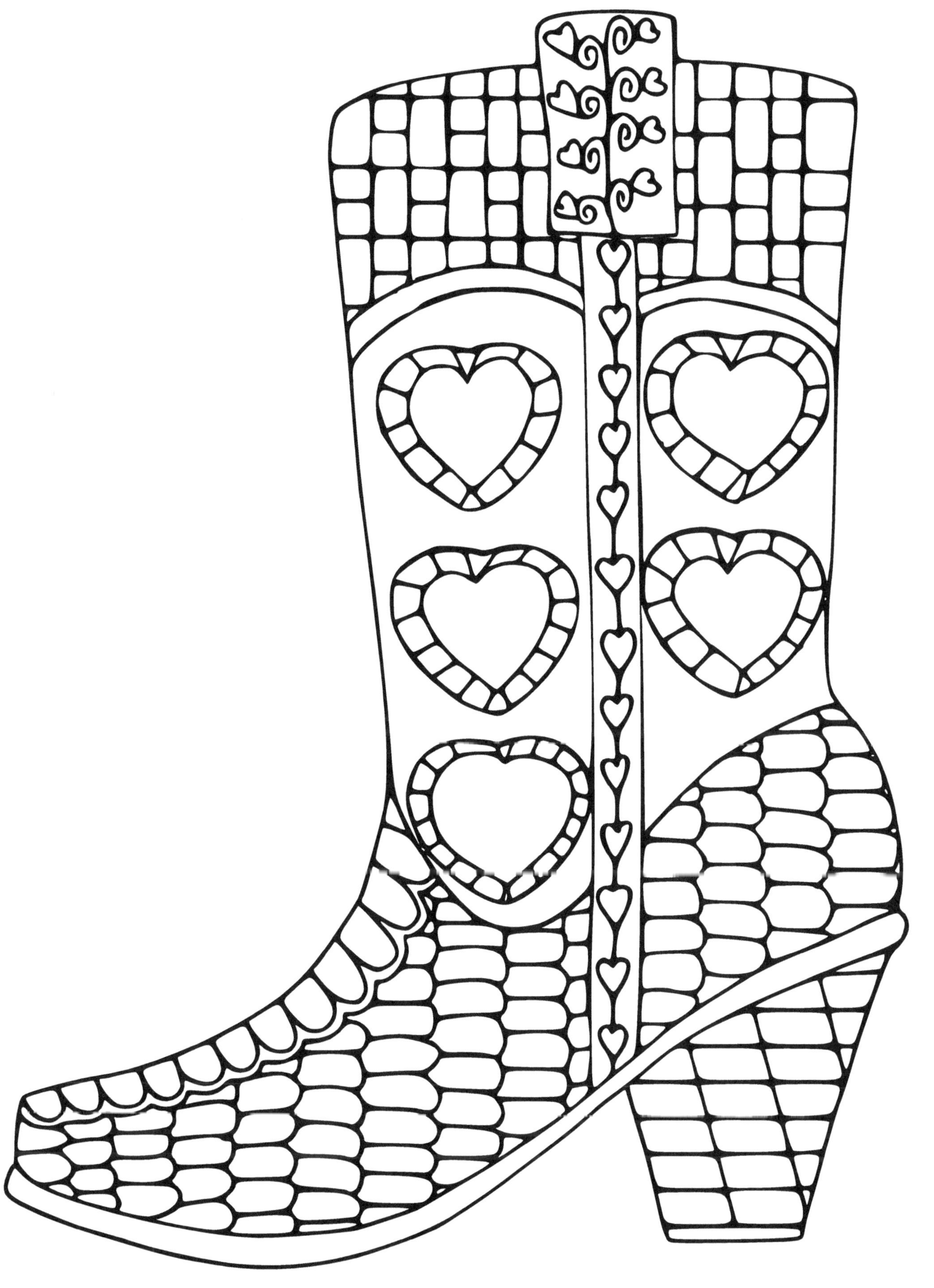

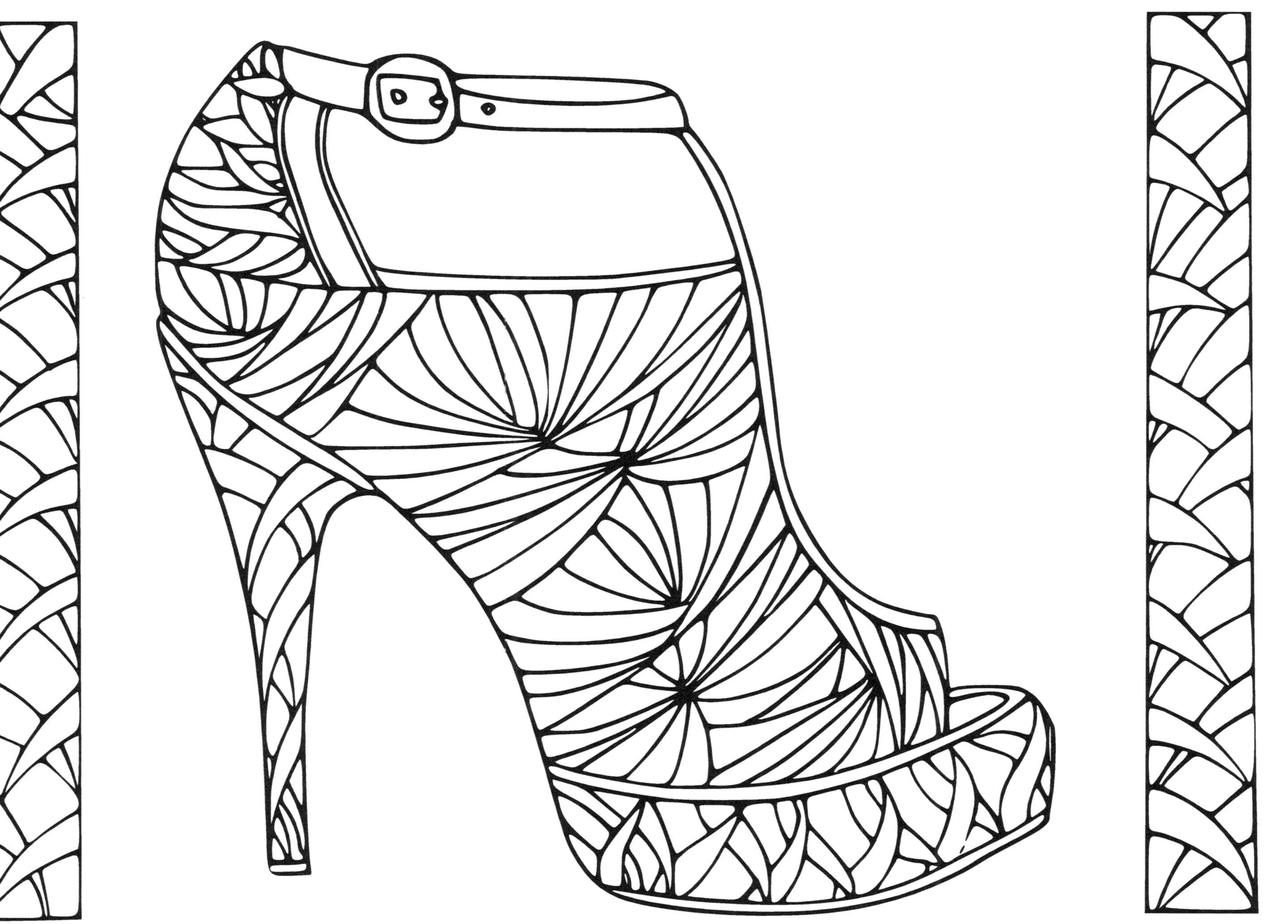

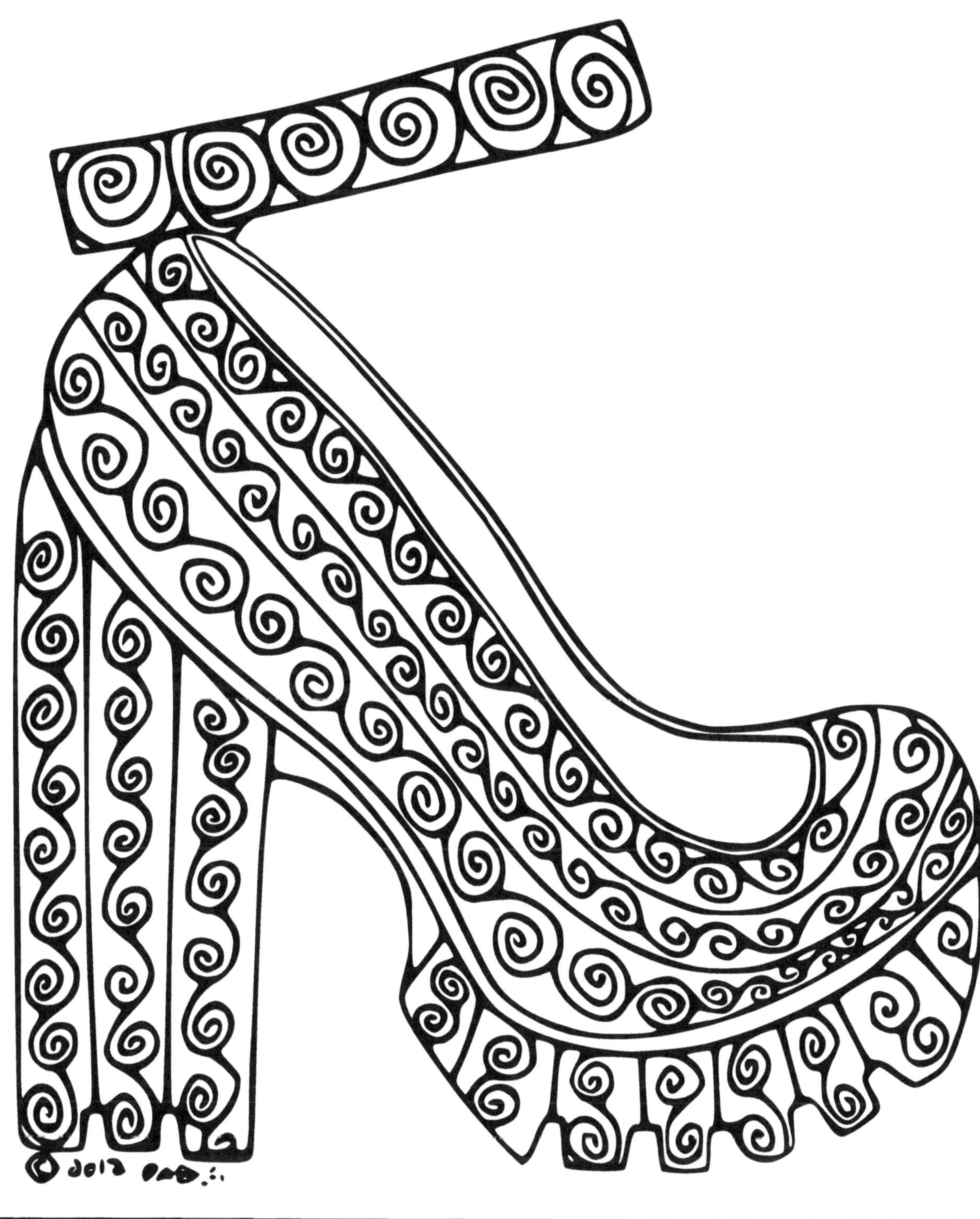

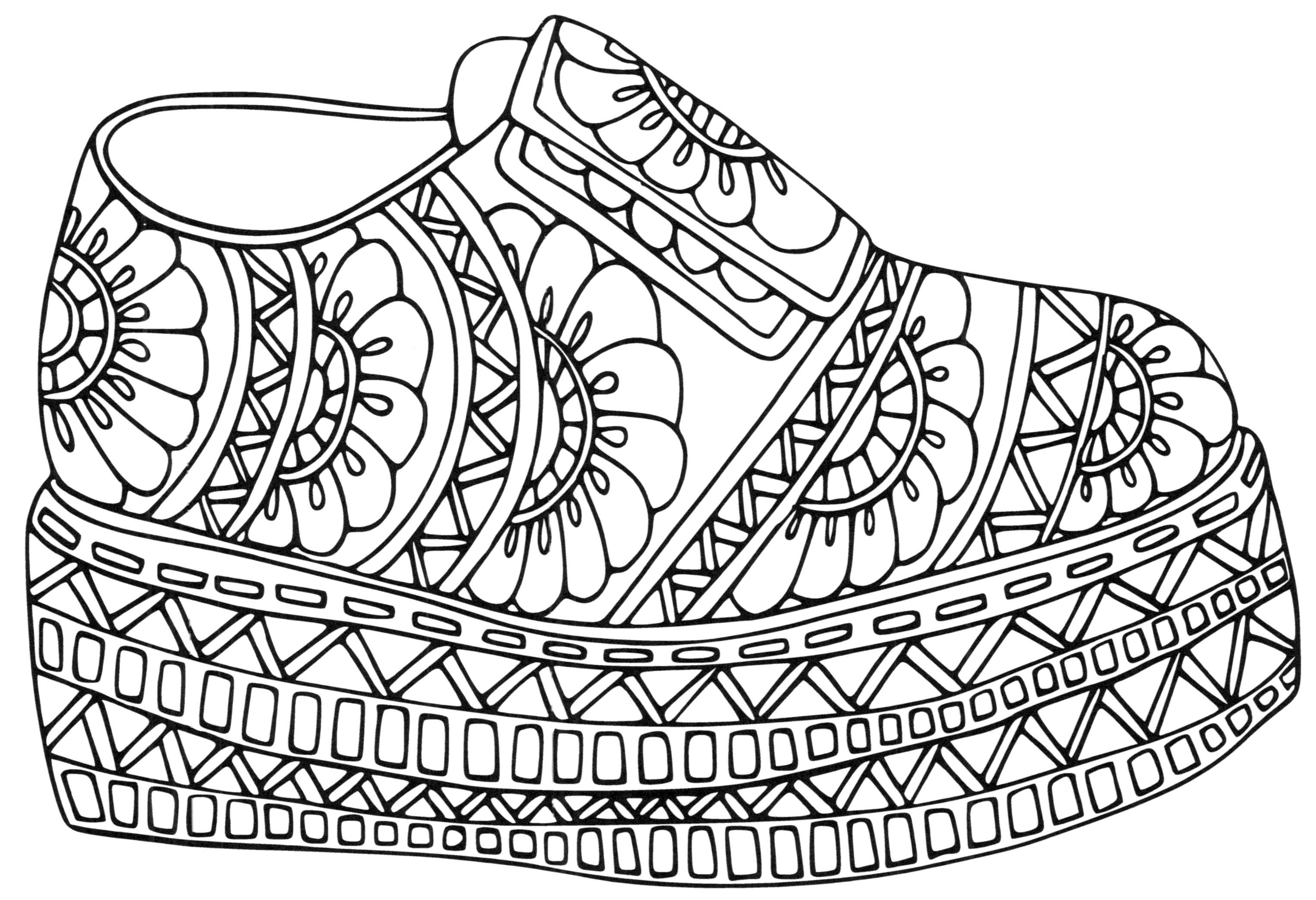

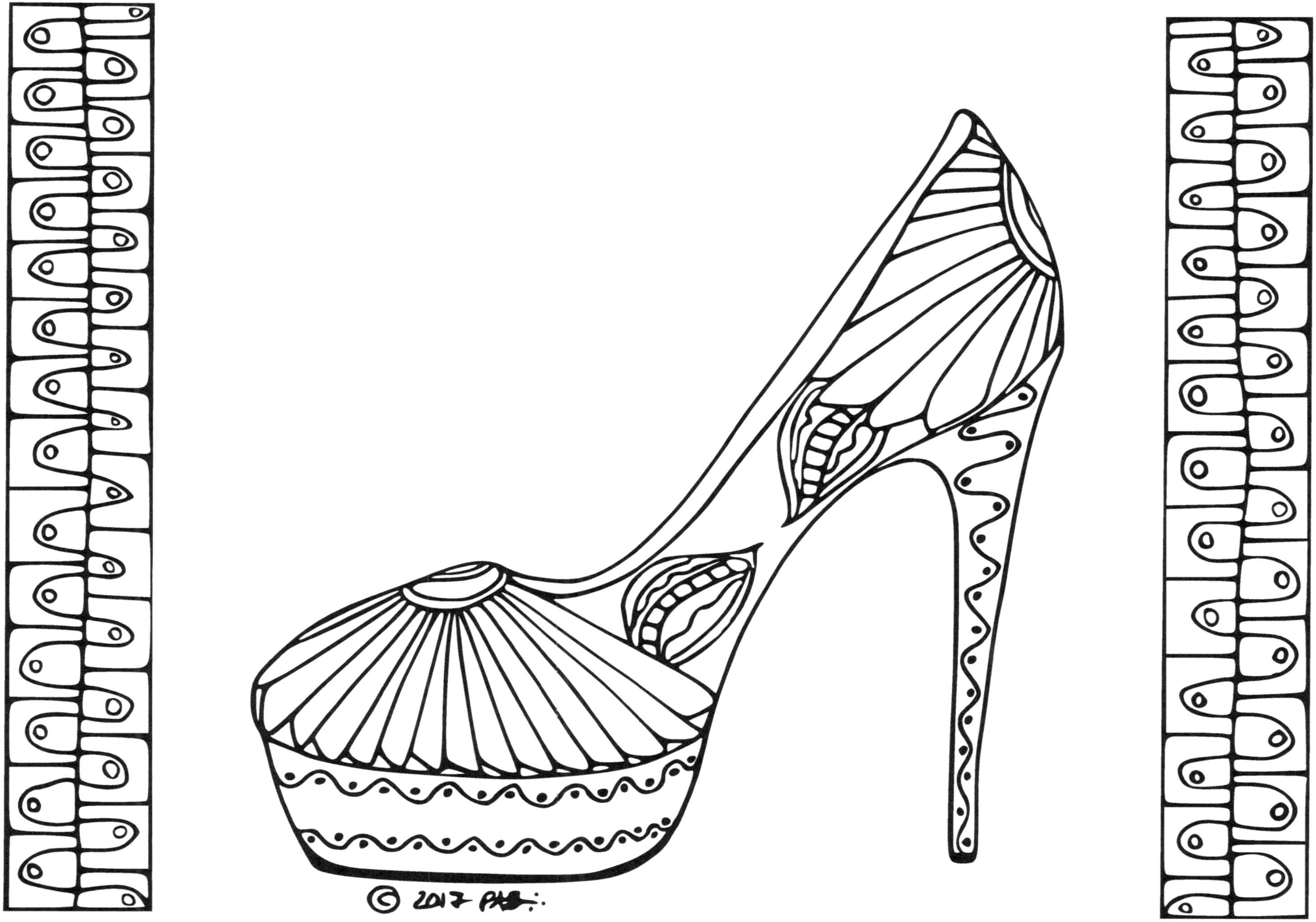

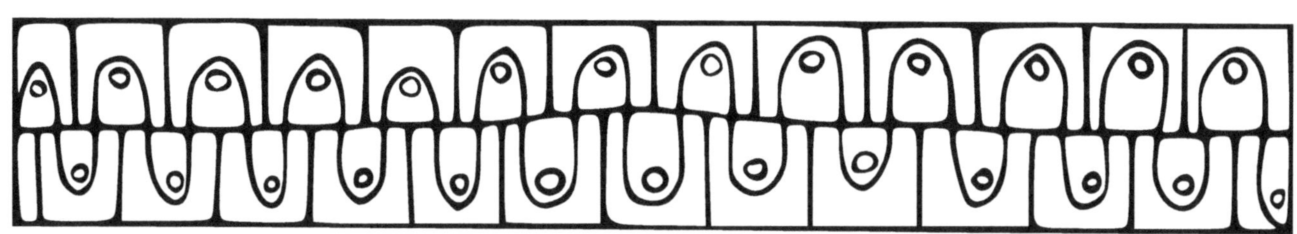

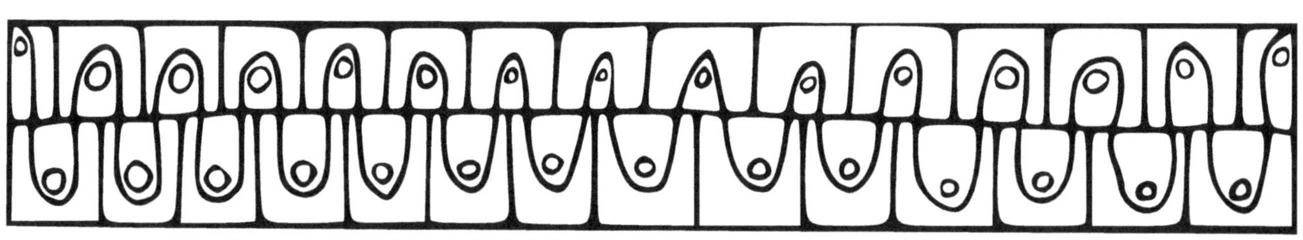

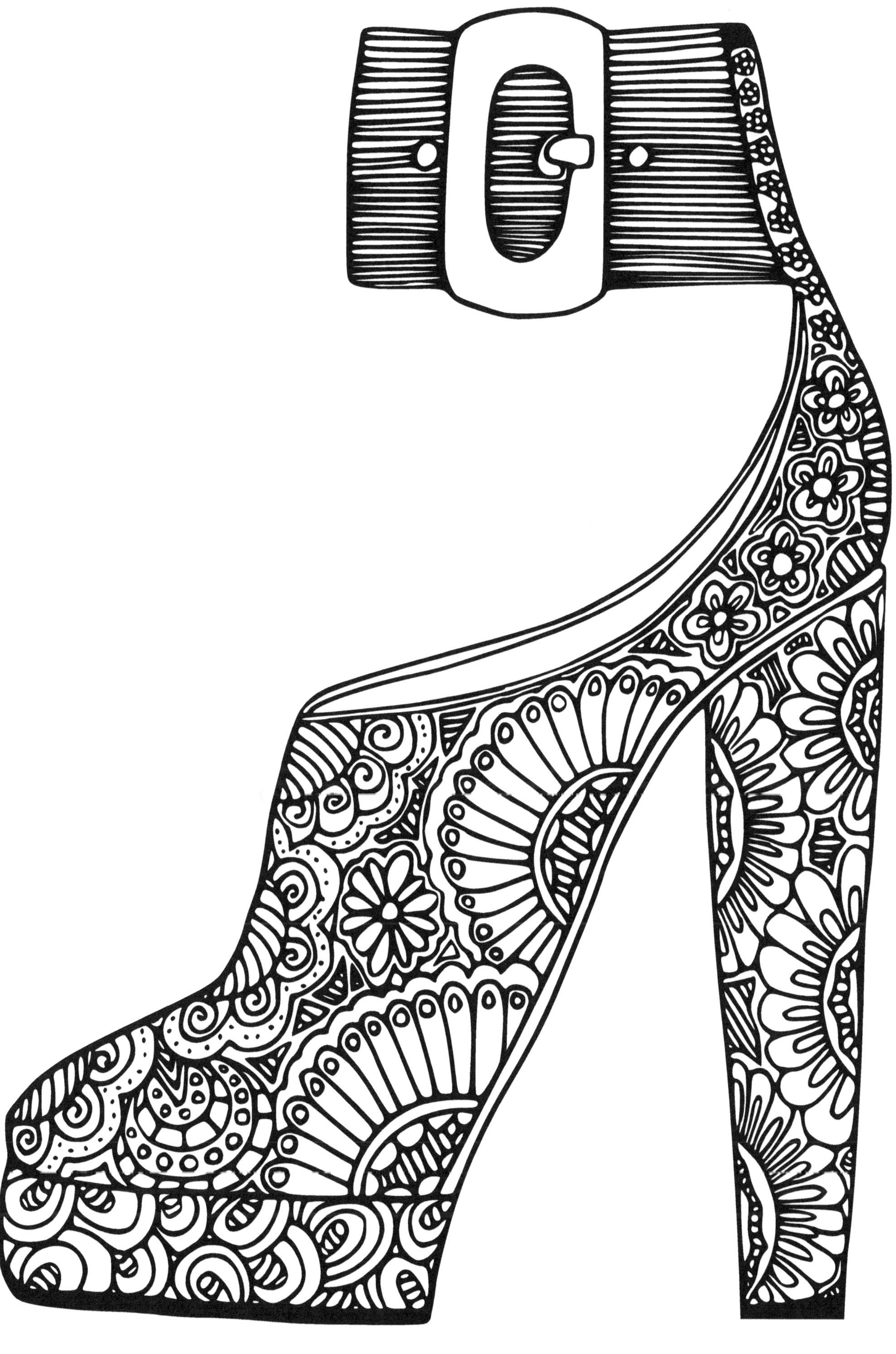

Blotter Page

Blotter Page

Blotter Page

www.ingramcontent.com/pod-product-compliance
Lightning Source LLC
LaVergne TN
LVHW081421110826
845149LV00010B/1828

* 9 7 8 0 9 9 7 5 9 5 9 5 6 *